In it for the Long Haul

The Fruit of Longsuffering

Dr. James E. McReynolds

Minister of Joy to the World

Parson's Porch Books

In it for the Long Haul: The Fruit of Longsuffering
ISBN: Softcover 978-1-960326-95-9
Copyright © 2024 by James E. McReynolds

Parson's Porch Books is an imprint of Parson's Porch *&* Company (PP*&*C) in Cleveland, Tennessee. PP*&*C is a self-funded charity which earns money by publishing books of noted authors, representing all genres. Its face and voice is **David Russell Tullock** (dtullock@parsonsporch.com).

Parson's Porch *&* Company *turns books into bread & milk* by sharing its profits with the poor.

www.parsonsporch.com

In it for the Long Haul

Contents

Dedication

To all the longsuffering servants of Jesus who have stayed the long haul despite the temptations to quit.

Even in the midst of harsh realities, there are always beautiful memories to celebrate gratitude.

"We cannot change the past, but we can change our attitude toward it. Uproot guilt and plant forgiveness. Tear out ignorance and seed humility. Exchange love for hate making the present comfortable And the future promising."

Maya Angelou

Foreword

Dr. John Killinger

Longsuffering. We're not good at it, are we? We usually know what we want, and we want it now. Not tomorrow, not the next day, not sometime in the future. NOW, in screaming immediacy.

My wife Gloria and I had a long visit this afternoon with some of her grandchildren and their children. One of those children, a cute little toddler named Kaizen, is four years old and accustomed to having his way—and having it when he wants it

He is well accustomed to turning up his volume to unpleasant levels if he isn't getting it, so the parents usually let him have it. "No, Kaizen," they say, "you can't have that," or "You can't do that." But then the din begins, and they soon weaken and capitulate.

It happen again and again. First, he was denied, but he soon was placated. And sadly, most children today are that way. It is easy to predict what they will be like as adolescents and young adults.

So this excellent book is a timely one. Extremely. And is in fact overdue.

My overwhelming impression, as I read it in manuscript form, was that it simple oozes with patience—and learning to delay one's gratification with developing an ability to hang on through things for the long haul, with developing the capacity to wait, to endure, and eventually to overcome.

Ours is not a waiting culture, unfortunately. It is always hurrying to get somewhere, to acquire whatever is desired, to reach its goals from the very moment they are identified.

Why is this? It wasn't this way when I was just a boy—though that was many years ago. People used to be a lot more patient. They understood that they had to wait and pray and work for the things they wanted or needed.

9

My mother wanted a dishwashing machine, but our family lived in three different homes before she finally got one.

I remember how proud of it she was, and how she loved to show it to her neighbors and to hear them say how wonderful it was, especially when many of them stood longing for the ones they hoped someday to possess.

Life is not that way any longer. Now the credit unions and production companies have persuaded most of us as that we don't have to wait, that whatever we want is ours the minute we can conceive of having the object of our irresistible desire delivered to our door before we can say, "Jack be nimble, Jack be quick."

This book is about tempering our resolves, learning to wait patiently in the midst of rushing, never temperament world, and finding joy and meaning in the self-control it advises us to develop.

The author concludes that it has to do with "being fully human." I like that. We discover our deep and true humanity as we learn to control our impulses and let life flow peacefully and uninterruptedly around us, without giving way to the feverishness of society and the harried pace of a world gone mad.

I confess I needed this book and its reminder of how life and desire can so easily spin out of control when we don't resolve to wait and observe and let things unfold at their own pace, without any help or impetus from us. I have really needed to slow down and smell the roses.

I needed to let my journey to unfold at its own deliberate pace, and to enjoy the love, the friendships and the opportunities it brings in its own sweet time.

I'll be better able to do it now.

This book says that, in the end, it's all about love—about waiting and savoring existence and counting our blessings. Life is full and beautiful without being pushed and tormented to yield its blessings before their time.

"God so loved the world"—and God has given us settings of untold beauty and value, if we only have the patience to see them.

I believe that. And now that I have this wonderful book to return to from time to time, I shall be much better to remember it and to live by it.

Dr. John R. Killinger, Warrenton, Virginia

Chapter One

Longsuffering: Growing Through Trouble

The fourth fruit of the Spirit is longsuffering according to Paul. Writing this book is the reader's invitation to experience the presence of God, even when life is not going the way we thought it would. You need not try to clean yourself up and hide. Paul's vision and his willingness to suffer patiently. Longsuffering helps us hope in the midst of pain. It responds to life with positive intentions. It brings deeper relationships during times of tension. It is our invitation to choose gratitude. It will shaper our spiritual senses. It shines with the unconditional love of God.

Longsuffering is having or showing patience in spite of troubles. A young woman who heard me preach on longsuffering said, "Pastor, that's one fruit of the Spirit I want to avoid." God uses seasons of longsuffering to build our patience and faith. We experience God as our Provider. Healer. Peace. Rock. Our Banner. Our Father. Weeping endures for the night, but the end of the season of longsuffering will come. Palm 30:5.

Charles Spurgeon said, "A Christian is the most contented person in the world, but least contented with the world." Romans 12:12.

Spurgeon also said, "Patience is a pearl which is found only in the deep seas of affliction, and only grace can find it there, bring it to the surface, and adorn the neck of faith with it." James 5:7-11.

When other people seal our joy, we are letting them steal our lives. Our goal for the years that remain in our lives is to experience eternal joy. The second part of our lives can be the best part of our lives. It is fruitless to attempt to understand others. Our lives are precious to us. We will stumble at times and find ourselves reverting back to old patterns. (Janet Van dewalle, *Women's Edition*, p. 64)

God uses everything for our good. I have learned the beauty of longsuffering. Lamenting shows trust in our Lord. This is extra ordinating considering the tragedies of life. Longsuffering shows us that God is in control. Our laments keep us engaged with God. We invite God into our pain. We will know our Creator's comfort and we create visions toward living in the Spirit. Joy is an echo of the presence of God. God does not hold past failures against us. Jesus said as much in the Sermon on the Mount. Matthew 5:7.

As Jesus promised, when we ask, we receive, as long as we do our part and ask in faith, believing God will answer. Matthew 21:21-22. Scripture shows how Jesus responds to unbelief. Mark 9:19-27.

It is normal for us to become impatient at Christ's delay in returning. We are triggered with even more impatience with the injustices that cause our longsuffering.

Lexicons and biblical commentaries reveal the meaning, "to be of a long spirit, not to lose heart, to persevere patiently in enduring misfortunes and troubles, to be patient in bearing the offenses and injuries from others."

Some people are called double-minded. That person is not able to give their self fully to God, because of heir love for the world. They want the best of two worlds. What I mean by double-minded is contrasted with the single mindedness of those who endure with long suffering. Double- minded people waver, whereas the faithful do not waver. They are not able to decide. Faithful ones are decisive.

They are unstable and lack conviction. They accept whatever sounds good. Un-threatening. Politically correct. Agreeable. Non-convicting. Convenient. I Timothy 6:18-19.

When we are being persecuted and we are in spiritual pain, rejoice that God will lift you up. Jesus gives a different perspective than the world does. As we used to sing around campfires, "They'll know we are Christians by our love."

When I encounter people living in nursing homes or care centers as their bodies begin to break down. We will not always be able to walk without assistance. Hearing must have an aid. They must depend on others to give them bites of food as they put it in your toothless mouth. We become helpless and humble. You will depend on God for your next breath. I Peter 1:3-9.

Longsuffering is weaving pain, passion, and grace. The vision quests for joy includes intentionally pacing people to intersect your journey while they are traveling on their own path as they encounter you. God transforms every situation so that there is an eternal focus. Do not be surprised that you will experience uncomfortable situations, mundane routine and unexpected challenges. No degree of temptation justifies any degree of sin.

Most modern translations use the word patience. I have about 300 translations of the Bible and most of them use "patience."

Patience is used in the *Living Bible, the Revised Standard Version, the New Revised Standard Version, Charles Williams Translation, Navarre Bible Commentary, Contemporary English Version, Amplified Bible, William Beck, New American Standard, Good News to Modern Man, Complete Bible by Edgar Goodspeed.*

Longsuffering is used in the *King James Version*. The archaic word long- suffering is seldom used today. I still like the way the *KJV* translates the original Greek which leads me to a deeper spiritual awareness.

Longsuffering is more than the ability to wait things out without getting angry. Some angry people are longsuffering. Longsuffering does not mean that human beings never get angry. We get angry at the right time, in the correct way, for correct reasons. This is as difficult as it is.

Greek words for patience generally refer to patience with people, situations, and tribulations or trials. Now think about the last time you got angry. Being set off unexpectantly causes angry responses. Longsuffering describes the difference between angry knee-jerks and an intentional decision for a specific purpose. I John 3:8-10.

I have consulted Hebrew and Greek lexicons, Bible commentaries, theological books, biblical dictionaries, concordances, and other sources to help me understand what to write. I have cited these in my bibliography at the end of this book.

I have never fully understood anger of a loving God. Love and anger are incompatible. God told Moses that mercy is always shown for the repenting ones. Exodus 34:6-7. David believe God as "good and ready to forgive" out of divine compassion, long-suffering, and grace. Psalm 86:5, 15. The Creator desires a relationship with us. That is the reason

15

God shows long-suffering when we fall short. Missing God's mark leas to the edge of divine long-suffering. We rejoices in forgiving our sins. Isaiah 43:25.

God is patient for a purpose. II Peter 3:9. God wants us to become part of the Father's family. Waiting as long as it takes, longer than any of us deserve. Isaiah 1:16-20. For us, long-suffering is taking a deep breath and looking at the bigger picture when we want to just lash out.

We exist to become children of God. Our family ordeal with cancer brought on encounters with people who did not understand. When my wife had to undergo chemotherapy, a few youth observed my now bald- headed wife in a grocery store. They stared at her smooth head. And then they yelled, "Did you see that lady? She doesn't have any hair. Gosh, that sure is ugly." My dear wife was living with breast cancer because the chemotherapy makes the hair fall out. It took much courage and longsuffering to go bald out in public. My wife debated what to do if that encounter happens again.

People suffering from cancer do double takes as they view themselves through glass windows or mirrors. Some become self-depreciated. They believe the lie, "I can only be beautiful with hair." Ordinary people see only the physical symptoms of a serious illness. Baldness is a side effect of something else. Sufferers see others that look prettier than them.

Chemo patients define a new normal of endless clinical procedures, scary machines, routine painful tests. God makes them brave to endure the road ahead. God makes them beautiful on the inside.

Longsuffering is to become strong in character

I have written and published books and preached many sermons on the first three fruit of the Spirit—love, joy, grace, and peace. I have also written on kindness and goodness. Long-suffering is first in the next group.

Longsuffering spirit-led people are not weak or meek. They are of strong character resisting rash reactions. II Peter 3:8-9. Peter reminds us of God's long-suffering in the days of Noah. I Peter 1:20.

Eternal tolerance is not the same as tolerance. Remember the warning of Galatians 6:7. Part of being Spirit-filled is long-suffering. Ephesians 4:2.

The problem today with the interest in becoming spiritual is that it is the result of a crisis situation as a quick fix to an immediate need. Once there is no longer a need, there is no longer the spirituality.

Real satisfying spirituality has a long hail view. Long term commitments enable Christians to endure despite any circumstances.

While preaching in Panama, I learned that Colonel George Washington Goethals was responsible for the completion of the Panama Canal. He was criticized for not completing the project. When asked if he wanted to respond to the critics, he said, "In time, when the canal is finished."

The call from God on our lives is for the long haul. The strength of spirituality is found in our long-term commitments, not the short-term experience.

The words from Paul teach us to develop a lifetime plan for spirit-filled living, not "flashing" spirituality. I Timothy 4:1-10. As the end of this era approaches, long-term commitments will be less frequent. There will be a falling out from faithfulness. I Timothy 4:1.

During these last days, the world will become filled with spirituality, but that spirituality focuses on extrabiblical teachings. When I served as an addiction therapist, many of my clients said they were spiritual but never religious. They scoffed off Christianity, but they did crazy things for a false kind of spirituality.

Some people will never read my books nor hear me preach as minister of joy to the world, but they pay literally thousands of dollars to hear some speaker from a flourishing cult. The real characteristics of spirituality will be known. Maturity cannot be faked.

We have a training program for most everything. We use education, professional insights, financial training, and athletic training. Paul emphasized to Timothy the need to train others. People's desire for being Spirit-filled will seek to purchase it like a financial package rather than through growing in discipleship.

No athlete becomes good without long-term training. No professional is allowed to work in his field without certification and training. Living the Christian life takes special effort. Spirituality never just drops into our laps from heaven.

In his letters to Timothy, Paul moves from proving the need to promoting the need. Most Christians agree that discipleship is needed, but how many in our modern congregations attend Sunday School. We need to teach by example and by preaching and teaching in public. A commitment to Christ needs tangible examples. Jesus helped us grasp this by coming to earth as a man. John 14:9. When we make any kind of commitment we are delighted and excited to do it.

Commitment Fruit and Our Time and Energy

With all the demands and pressures of society, we must be careful not to throw away the commitment we made to Christ. Long-suffering is a long haul. The fruit of a commitment to Christ requires lots of time.

Drops of rain can make a hole in stone by continuing to fall. Persevere and be tenacious with long term effort. The author of Hebrews teaches that in the scheme of things, long-suffering in a lifetime will be a small time compared to eternity. Hebrews 10:37. Long term faith will prevent our "shrinking back." Hebrews 10:39. We will finish well. We will die well.

Commitment and perseverance breeds passion, a fire that will not go out. Our task is to stir the flames of our desires with everything we possess.

In a commencement speech, I told the graduates that Louisa May Alcott was told she did not have the talent of writing anything that would appeal to any audience. An editor of a newspaper told Walt Disney had no good ideas. Beethoven was told by his music eacher tat he was hopeless as a composer. Carl Sandburg flunked out in English class.

His teachers called Einstein stupid in grade school.

Living in a world when we get most anything immediately has not prepared us well for the disciplines that are spiritual. Healthy spirituality requires a long-haul approach. There are no short cuts to become mature in the Spirit. Quality faith trumps quick fixes. The fourth fruit of the Spirit Listed in Galatians 5:22 is longsuffering. This fruit enables the first fruit, really all of them to continue despite hardships.

The gift of longsuffering is for responding to the ugly parts of our lives. God touches our hollow places. God sees your reflection in a mirror to reflect our truth worth. Whenever you focus on blemishes, God sees beauty. When you cringe at your baldness, God notices your courage.

"People look at our outward appearances, but the Lord looks at the heart." I Samuel 16:7. We embrace life in a fallen world. Psalm 139:23-24. We greet longsuffering with joy, James 1:2. Suffering incites our will to find meaning. Pain enables us to discover ourselves.

Embracing life, including its disappointments, as e hear the welcome of God. We are able to see how much ground must be traveled The horizon is beyond our reach.

God's vision for life embraces us with joy and strength. Love is a taste of life that is indescribable. Each human journey is as unique as a snowflake. Life is incomparable. We must walk our path alone. We are called to be like God.

The Gift of Joy

Joy is the best gift to increase energy and improve our health. Joy energizes us as this emotion mobilizes the body's production of endorphins. These are the same uppers that marathon racers feel. Joy increases our immunity to disease

Longsuffering is to know our encounters have derailed us is the key to our coming to grips with our sin. Our goal must be to live in tune with God's Spirit. The Spirit guides us in the most important decisions of our lives.

There is no substitute for the joy that is there when a follower of Jesus experiences loss or trouble. Joy comes with trouble. To live is to encounter trouble. Our fait tells us there is purpose in longsuffering. Pain is not meaningless. Trouble becomes necessary for joy.

One of the most difficult obstacles to celebrating life fully in pain. We fear and dread pain. Created for joy, we find suffering to be congruous with human tragedy. The apostle Paul knew trouble. He lived as a single man. Philippians 1: 12-14. Paul used his troubles to advance the gospel.

He never denies his suffering. He viewed his pain with a positive attitude. Paul had the end in mind. His goal was not to find comfort. He lived a Christ-centered life. Paul might have heard these words from Jesus in the Sermon on the Mount. Matthew 5:11-12. Paul expected suffering. Life in Christ comes with trouble.

Catherine Marshall, wife of Peter Marshall, said, "Few of us are challenged with the promise of soft living." From a prison cell in the city of Rome, Paul shared how to experience joy. John 15:11, Psalm 5:11. Paul had a secure mind. Paul knew his position was in Christ. Colossians 1:25- 27, John 15:1-7. Paul had a passion that could not be quenched. Romans 1:16, II Timothy 4:2, I Corinthians 1:18, 9:6. His purpose was higher than any other. Romans 8:29, Galatians 2:20.

Paul's suffering and service was his privilege. Missionary Jim Elliott said, "He is no fool to give what he cannot keep to gain what he cannot lose." God has more to do with the dynamics of longsuffering than we do. We must do first things first. Longsuffering is at the base of our commitment. Joy is the residue of experiencing living love and grace. Joy will happen with a steady, long-term relationship with God.

We need not hide the cracks and flaws that we have. We are God's workmanship, and we have nothing to hide. Our sanctification will enable us to withstand the heat and pressure of living. Philippians 1:12.

Salvation is God's work from beginning until the end. God causes all things to work together for good to those who love God, to those called according to God's purpose. Romans 8:28. God desires to complete the work that has been full of difficult circumstances, which can decimate faith, use up our energy, and only the brave will survive. A believer will face the stiffest of oppositions, pressing encounters, and continue to brave them. We must go through many tribulations to enter the kingdom of God. Acts 14:22. Suffering brings our salvation into clear focus. We gain assurance that we are citizens of heaven living on inside the hostile earth.

The weaker we are, the more clearly the grace of God will shine. Our humility and brokenness reveals the continuous faith and grace. The people in the midst of longsuffering have the empowering of the Spirit.

Joy comes to humble people. Humility means that one has an accurate self-concept. Philippians 2:1-4. Paul sensed the unity of the believers. Their one mind was the mind of Christ. Their one love was the love of Christ. The followed one Spirit, the Spirit of Christ. They had one purpose, the purpose of the Father. With brave courage, a believer faces the stiff oppositions and pressing circumstances. They trust the sovereignty of a loving God. We rejoice in our salvation.

God's desire for us is to be aware that most thinking people, theologians, and seers agree that God has a universal will binding on each one. We are to live in harmony with our human nature. We must then correct our reasoning. Living according to the teachings and examples of Jesus is the will of God. Jesus shows us how God wants us to live. In our many personal choices, we cannot say that we have found God's will. Humility brings joy.

God gave us the desire to enjoy things in life. Life would be boring without this desire. Our desires are good as long as we fulfill them within the plan and rules of God. Improper satisfaction of a natural desire is an instance of a lust in the flesh. Desire actually means "a lust after that which is forbidden."

Fulfillment in the Christian life comes as we bear fruit to the glory of God. We are elated when the fruit of others who received faith through our example and invitation are the goals of those with the mind of Christ.

God gave us the desire to accomplish things. We all desire this, but we must do it within God's direction or it becomes more sin. God doesn't tempt us We tempt ourselves. We intentionally put ourselves in places of temptation. There is a mysterious thrill in nurturing a temptation. We do not realize when we have crossed the line. The Greek word is "to catch by bait." If one wants to catch an animal, you lure it out with some kind of bait. Once the animal sees the bait, it gets closer and closer. It is no longer safe. He bait looks and smells wonderful. So the creature is seduced successfully. It is then subject to harm and even death.

Dramatic private revelations

We reflect on our encounters and experiences as indications of God's will. I am not saying that this divine will comes from dramatic private revelations. This is not God's normal method of communicating this will. God desires us to be freed from all influences on our decision that do not come from the Spirit.

Culture and immediate environment are huge influences. We are also influenced by our own dividedness. This is the tension between ourselves and the Holy Spirit. What is tempting to one person is not tempting to another. Not every hook sinks in. Sin is a conscious act. Once we are seduced into the darkness, we could live there forever. A Spirit-filled Christian resists temptation. The testing makes us stronger. The Christian will ask for forgiveness. When we fall, as everyone sometimes does, we take responsibility for the sin. I Corinthians 10:13.

Place that verse on your bathroom mirror., put it inside your wallet, or in the visor of your automobile. Remember Jesus was tempted just as we are. Temptations are something every human being encounters.

One day we shall understand every trial that entered our lies God's single- minded nature makes all things work for our good. Scripture tells us how we need to respond in our experiences. We are commanded to react to the world around us in a caring, loving, and affirming way. We must do the opposite of what a natural self will do.

God gives positive redirection. Be quick to listen. We may hear the sound of a caring person but we are concentrating on other things. It is not in our nature to listen well. Be aware of our problem and decide to make an effort.

Another important thing is for us to be slow to speak. We ere created with one tongue and two ears for a reason. We are to close our mouths. We say things that cannot be taken back. We do more harm than good. Note the truth: "If you don't have anything good to say, don't say anything." Romans 12:18-21. Just because some people are yelling and trying to hurt you, there is no reason for us to act in kind.

The apostle John summarized it in his small letter. John 2:15-17. We are to free ourselves from the lust of the world. John is saying that we are not Christians if we continue on.

Lay aside the world. Pick up and accept the Word. The Word was planted in us. Love the world but do it with humility and meekness. We accept all God's Word, not just the parts we choose.

Replace your wisdom with God's wisdom. The world's way of thinking with God's way of thinking. God's thoughts are not our thoughts.

God's Word will penetrate our hearts and souls leading us into action. We must not deceive ourselves. James 1:23-24. The reward for being a doer is a surprising blessing Notice what Jesus told us. John 8:31-32. This was also Paul's theme in Romans. 8:2.

This incredibly important command is to lay aside the world, accept the Word, do the Word. I John 3:18. That would be an effective outline for your next sermon if you are a preacher. James 1:26-27.

Serving others always requires sacrifice. Jesus set the example. Imagine the joy of sharing your relationship with Christ with another person and helping them become faithful. Imagine the joy of seeing someone who taught as their mentor became a peer with you.

Living with love, grace, joy, and peace requires paradox. Our gains become losses. We must realize that we ae powerless to live successfully on our own abilities. Joy comes as we trust God. We are being what God wants us to be. We are doing what God wants us to do. We are going where God wants us to go.

Human beings do not have to look far to experience hard times. We need not be overwhelmed. We can choose to be part of the solution of God to the pain and suffering of this word.

"If we do nothing and remain silent and in the face of oppression of others,

we will learn by looking in a mirror and observe humans being taken away to be slaughtered."

Marty Janzglass

Chapter Two

Longsuffering in Black Culture

For part of my doctoral study in worship, preaching, and literature, I was blessed to take a course on Black Preaching. Henry Mitchell directed our study at Vanderbilt University Divinity School.

We read a helpful book entitled *Soul Theology*. Mitchell said the essential of African American faith is longsuffering. He called it the perseverance of the saints. In spite of trials, troubles, and struggles, they believed they could overcome. Unemployment lines were long. Money to pay bills was short. Longsuffering intensified black people. They kept saying, "If you can take it, you can make it."

Every culture is given social identities. Even today, dominant races bestow benefits to themselves. In my notes from the Black Preaching course, African Americans experience longsuffering with disadvantages, disapproval, and limitations. This means they are oppressed by institutional power and discrimination.

Social identity is internally established and externally applied. Oppression has caused deep suffering. It divides communities who should be working together.

The entire human race have differing identities, but all eight billion of us are connected. Conversations are needed to develop deeper understanding to prevent more harm.

The struggles of black people are referenced in songs. Spiritual songs have now become popular music songs.

They suffered humiliation. They were sent to jails and prisons for petty crimes. African Americans dared to believe they could persevere and endure in spite of how they had been treated as slaves. They continued to sing, "Done made my vow to the Lord, and I never will turn back. I will go, I shall go to see what the end will be."

The end for most African Americans has been positive. The number of black university professors more than tripled between 1970 and 1990. Better and higher paying jobs now exists. The recent death of

George Floyd has expedited new laws and reformed police methods. Floyd's death exposed the unhealed wounds of the past. The Black Lives Matter Movement has spread to all areas of American culture.

A human being is a human being no matter the color of the skin, their gender, or economic class.

Burden of the People

Teaching such as Mitchell spoke of should be a requirement of ministers. Afterwards and during the course, I wrote a book titled *Black Preaching: Burden of a People*. It was published with the help of a man from the First Baptist Church of Nashville, the African American one. Working at a printing shop, he published 1,000 copies which we gave to African and European Americans.

Resource for the study of preaching

The book is listed as a resource for the study of preaching. Thoughts in the book have been quoted in many sermons. Regardless of life's imprisonments, God will be with us. The reality of longsuffering is that patience is what we are left with when we lose dignity and freedom. The faithful Spirit-filled soul cries out, "How long, Lord, how long."

When my wife suffered from breast cancer, she lost her feel to play the piano through neuropathy from the chemical treatments. She learned the power of waiting. Isaiah 40:31.

Longsuffering was a core belief for African Americans. They believed patience was the soul of perseverance. They suffered long when their path was rough with unmovable mountains to climb. Longsuffering tells us that when hopelessness has reached its worst, when there is nowhere to turn, God will not leave us comfortless.

The power and importance of longsuffering might be revealed as love, grace, and joy precede longsuffering. This fruit prepares people for that moment when the freedom bells ring.

In my travels to black nations my calling as the minister of joy to the world has brought evidence of black joy. Simultaneous expressions of deep sorrow and hopeful moments of joy are an endearing and enduring part of today's black culture.

Those who fought for voting rights in 1965 sang joyful freedom songs as they marched from Selma to Montgomery, Alabama, despite violence and harassment. This was a picture of sharing joy amid sorrow. They imagined what could be possible.

Living with justice and joy the strong people dreamed bigger. My friends and fellow students at Vanderbilt Divinity School cultivated black joy. My black friends had life visions with hope for tomorrow. They had transformative imaginations of what could be if we all worked together.

Some of the black students saw black joy as essential part of the vision quests in the work for dignity despite the obstacles that come from living in an atmosphere that disdained blacks. Illustrations of joy brought moments of strength and love that most of us continue to recall. I call it sanctified suffering. African Americans focused on living hope. They lived for eternity. They became full citizens in heaven as strangers in the hostile world. Their lives illustrated the joy in suffering. Despite their fiery trials, they knew they had an eternal destiny and a heavenly destiny.

African Americans deserve the right to experience life with all its potential. White joy, black joy, red and yellow joy is essentially the same. Joy is the unfiltered ability to go on the scared journey to enjoy the goodness of life. Trials involved their focus on faith. Their joys were intensified not extinguished. Of course, their trials caused grief and longsuffering. They lived for eternity. They escaped from the futility of the human condition.

The African American path to glory winded through troubling times and intense suffering. Their faith was refined and focused on Jesus Christ. Imagine how life would be for people of color if they had no vision of eternity. They made a strong commitment and they were willing to pay a price. Romans 8:18. The price made them not coast through life or exhibit spiritual sluggishness. Their amazing high character impacted their conduct. Looking to the character of Jesus, they refused to live in fear because eternity meant accountability.

As professor Christopher Meadows said, "Joy is recognizing there is a problem and continuing to focus on standing up and doing something to live in longsuffering that moves us forward."

The conduct of suffering people is commendable. Slaves lived in a fishbowl environment. They had a maligned reputation. Their common unselfish objectives were slandered, even through they submitted to every authority. Some enslaved people had a teachable rather than a defensive spirit even when corrected or given instructions. They kept a respectful attitude. Some endured with patience. Others ran away.

Their quiet and meek spirit. It was the only kind of attitude in light of their context. It was remarkable that some were more concerned about the eternal destiny of those persecuting them than the inhuman problems of those in control. Christ demonstrated this to the ultimate degree when he shouted from the Roman cross, "Father, forgive them for they know not what they do."

We are to do nothing out of favoritism. I Timothy 5:21. The book of James gives us insight. James 2:1-7. James refers to his readers as brothers. All races are to be knit together. Part of the solution is for us to be believers in Jesus Christ. We can share that in common. The biblical word for favoritism means "to accept a face." Being completely fair and impartial is difficult in our world. I Samuel 16:7.

God wants us to totally disregard outward appearances, and as the savior of the world tells not to judge by outward things but the heart of a persons, whoever they are.

A person's self-worth is the foundation of black joy. Joy mixes in to make African Americans who they are. Joy gives spaces and encounters where people are there to lift you. Joy is a form of reparation and comfort.

Envisioning the future, black joy will continue to be cultivated in the path ahead of us. Joy exists in moments, in honoring the best of the past, in the large and small, the ordinary and the extraordinary, that allow people to live as themselves. That is the goal in our longsuffering world. Minimize things that divide us.

God wants us to look at the things that bind us together. We need to change our attitude. Realize that racism is simply ignorance. Too many people of all races base their opinions on outward appearances. Their foundation for giving us all more burdens is prejudice or instituted by social status is wrong.

We can rise above that. Look around you. Experience the whole world and see it for what it is. Look to Jesus as your example. Look to God for wisdom and understanding. If we put God's Word and our words into action, there will be peace and joy and love now and always. Just do it.

Commendable conduct enables us to escape the futility of the human condition. We must be harmonious as we think the same. Feeling together makes us sympathetic. Loving one another like sisters and brothers. Being humble in spirit and quick to show and feel affection.

God's grace is calling us and blessing us. We must think straight, sensibly, and seriously. This is not in ignorance and frivolity. Like-minded people live free from excess, rashness, passion, confusion. Thinking straight is the key foundation for us. "Take time to be holy, speak oft (often) with the Lord; forgetting in nothing his blessing to seek."

Love covers a multitude of sins. Sins require our addressing them. As we get to know each other well and live in neighborhoods fervently loving one another.

Mutual ministry is the responsibility of all believers. Together we benefit the whole body of Christ. Sacred sacrifice is involved. We are the pipeline for the resources of God. Pass them on. An African Methodist Episcopal minister reflected on the idea of his predominately black congregation join the United Methodist Church. "We aren't going," he said. "The United Methodist Church is losing members and churches because of conflict and differing opinions. I shall stand strong by the grace of God where I am."

Encouraging all black, white, or any colored denomination to realize that present hardships are not worthy of being compared wit the future glory and the rewards for coming together in mutual faithfulness. We must function as a team. Remember the kingdom is composed of the "flock of God," not one group or denomination.

The proper style of ecumenical leadership is not compulsion, but leadership by example.

"As long as the candle is still burning, it is still possible to accomplish and to heal."

Old Jewish proverb

Chapter Three

Longsuffering Moves Mountains

Spirit-filled people do things that are impossible with the fruit, the gift of longsuffering. Mountain moving faith begins with a dream. Martin Luther King declared, "I have a dream." He was given imagination. Every success begins with a dream.

Paint a picture in your mind about what you want to accomplish. Reject the thoughts of impossibility. Desiring something different comes with longsuffering. We desire something so intently somehow, somewhere, sometime, the impossible happens. Make your mental picture with details and dates.

Perhaps lack of courage, fear of embarrassment, rejecting high risks are reasons you do not move your personal mountains. Longsuffering means more than a dream or desire. Longsuffering causes us to risk failure. Every time we make a choice, we are at risk.

Grace, love, joy, peace rides along with longsuffering generates soul excitement, enthusiasm, energy so that we can now begin. Mountain movers begin to act as if nothing will make the dream fail.

Longsuffering is a powerful gift for success. If you expect success, then you will hold nothing back. Unlike the rich young ruler, you will give your last dollar, spend your second wind energy, and gamble your reputation, confident that you will make it after all.

A Nebraska woman whose son was in Ukraine was not worried about her son. I am calm and he'll be just fine. She boldly predicted success in his brave adventure.

Every adventure will go through a period of time when a problem is overwhelming. Remind yourself of Jesus' words about moving mountains. Sometimes there is nothing to do but wait.

We shall experience situations when our mountain does not move despite all we do. Undergoing longsuffering, we must surrender, let go and let God help you move the mountain. Mark 11:22-23.

Fill all your senses with faith in God. Use the inner ear John 5:30. Receive God's strength. Genesis 12:1-3. Use the inner eye. Revelation 4:1. Receive God's vision. Genesis 15:5-6. Use the inner mind. Luke 2:19. Ponder the thoughts of God. Romans 4:20-21. Use the inner will. Acts 19:21, Genesis 17:5.

Moving mountains is a journey into the unknown. We travel the dark valley with difficulty and suffering. We must refine the vision. We will feel joy coming alive. Rain softens earth in joyful surprises. Winter is kissed by light. Joy is the guiding light in our personal firmament.

Life is not elsewhere. It is living in you. Life is a marathon and not a short sprint. We run with endurance. Hebrews 10;36. We learn to endure by enduring. Stand firm, be reliable and immovable. Finish well for the glory of God in Christ. Faith and faithfulness are keys to endure in longsuffering.

For the long haul, we must throw away some things. These hinder us. We are required to throw off "the sin that so easily entangles us. Hebrews 12:1. An unwavering commitment is required to run the race. We must be willing to run. Hebrews 11:6, Isaiah 40:30-31. We run with perseverance. Hebrews 11:1-40, 12:1, Romans 4:18. We run with purpose. I Corinthians 9:26, Psalm 37:23.

Endurance comes from God. Romans 15:5. Winston Churchill said in the middle of World War II, "Hard times bring out the best in people, and the worst."

Faith gives us mountain moving power. Matthew 17, Mark 11. Jesus used physical illustrations to communicate faith. "Tell this mountain to be cast into the sea" were Jesus' words to instruct his disciples. This incredible promise of mountain moving occurs in the context of purity and prayer.

Readers, please look at when and where Jesus shared his astonishing words. He is talking about the spiritual nature of God's kingdom. There is a vast world beyond our senses. II Corinthians 4:18.

The terminology of moving mountains elevates out perception beyond the limits of time and place. It is the spoken expression of believing in God and speaking our faith into action.

In our lifetime journeys, we face mountains. Your marriage could be a mountain. Financial mountain. Health mountain. We pray about the mountains. We pray God will remove fear. When we face a mountain, we feel we are asking God in vain.

Some mountains must be commanded, spoken to, and told what to do. It is not just a coincidence that God chose a mountain to represent our problems. Mountains seem to be permanent. Jesus told us that if we are going to see a mountain move, we must command it in the authority of God.

Following Jesus is learning how to use the authority that God gives us. We are given mountain-moving faith. Moving mountains is God given. It is for the glory of God, not ours. It is God who wants this mountain to move. We cannot move a mountain that e want removed in our own power.

Not every mountain we speak to will be removed. God works through people. Our Creator wants us to participate in these removals. God desires that we experience the power flowing through us.

Once Saved, Always Saved

In evangelical settings, the phase, "Once saved, always saved," was shared in an old story abut grace and the perseverance of the saints. He said he was going to a barber to get a haircut and a shave. He had been doing it by himself and with the help of his wife. So he drove to the shop owned by a Baptist preacher. That day the pastor was out, so his wife Grace did the job. After doing the work, Grace said, "That will be $30."

When he went home, he studied his look, and he really liked what he saw in the mirror. He stopped the barber shop to tell Grace and told her, "It had been two weeks and I still have no stumble on my face. I thought your price was high. Grace looked at him and said, "You were saved by Grace. Once shaved, always shaved."

During my spiritual pilgrimage, my theological understanding was that once we were saved, we were always saved. I heard it often, especially when I heard a sermon from John 10:27-30. My view was too limited and too broad. Some used the phrase as a license to sin, a transaction that means no commitment was needed. It was the basis for those who taught an extreme Calvinism. God just moved our mountain of lostness. Others sled into an extreme Arminianism where a person was so free that she or he can fall in and out of salvation. Grace has no power.

Progress in the spiritual life depends on the Holy Spirit. We are "to go on to perfection." Hebrews 6:1-6. The biblical teaching is tat nothing can separates us from the love of God. Left to ourselves alone, we would be in danger of falling away. I Corinthians 9:24-27.

Sometimes the saved and the unsaved, the regenerated and the unregenerated. Matthew 13:24-30. Humans cannot distinguish the tars from the wheat.

Baptists wrote the New Hampshire Confession of Faith in 1833 gave the words, ". . . such only are only believers as endure to that end their persevering attachment to Christ is the grand mark of their salvation."

Salvation is our active cooperation with the grace of God. It depends on God's strength not ours. Luke 10:27. When we realize our completely lost state, that is the time when God does something amazing.

It describes the depth of the mercy of God. We do not deserve it. We can never earn it. God chooses to bestow this marvelous gift in redemption, love, and grace. James 2:2-13. All of God's people will show mercy, because they have been given mercy.

Longsuffering is the fruit to measure your faith and your faithfulness. We will be filled with confidence in the Spirit. We will understand faith and the reality of our eternal salvation. Ephesians 2:1-10. Look inside your heart and ask God to help you develop a fruitful relationship that produces good deeds, compassion, love, and forgiveness.

In writing about longsuffering I know that I have put my oar in a large sea. All I can do within my limits is to row out on this sea as far as I am able.

We are declared righteous in the courtroom of heaven. Justification does not mean "make just" but "to declare just." Christ lived a perfect divine life and he died an obedient death. Romans 5:19, 10:4, II Corinthians 5:21, Philippians 3:9, Ephesians 1:7. Justification is by faith alone. This is the rock where we stand in the midst of longsuffering. Justification is by grace, not by our merit but on Christ alone.

We confuse justification and sanctification. God gives us the Holy Spirit and transforms us into the image of Christ. The progressive change is not justification. The change is sanctification. Romans 6:22.

With empty hands we received Christ whose faithful life of love perfectly filled the law of God. By faith alone we are united with Christ. This is justification.

Sanctification is by faith alone. Only faith receives the power to receive the fruit of love. Sanctification matters. Sanctification is the evidence that the seed of the Christian life is in our soul. It makes a huge difference for us to become assured in our longsuffering of our own imperfection. We have a perfect righteousness outside ourselves in Christ.

God will never turn us away. John 6:37. The light will rise in due time. God will hold on to us. Jude 24. This is the promise of God. Romans 8:30. Glory is coming. II Corinthians 4:17-18.

David shared his own experience of patiently waiting. Psalm 40:1-3. He is living in "the pit of destruction." The song of praise and glory, but it is not there yet. Psalm 69:1-2. David combined the images of "mud" and "flood." In his pit of mud and destruction, he felt helpless and desperate It is a beautiful when a broken man genuinely cries out to God. Psalm 6:6, 56:8.

The prophet Micah experienced prolonged and painful waiting. Micah 7:8-9. There are no deadlines for God. God's love is perfect for us. Our efforts to grasp the fullness of eternal joy in Christ are secure by Christ grasping us. This security rests on Christ's faithfulness.

Unconfessed Sin Clogs Joy.

The cause for longsuffering is our cherished sin that we will not let go. Sin is a barrier to joy. We are never to make light of sin. We do not have to continue to be overwhelmed. We have extended times of suffering because we are unwilling to renounce our sin. Matthew 5:23-24.

Unconfessed and unforsaken sin clogs our joy. Psalm 32:2-3. We are permitted to hold fast to our sin. We can keep it secret. We can groan all day long" in longsuffering. We must confess sin and enjoy the stunning experience of one whom the Lord counts no iniquity.

Think deeply about the unconscious depravity in our souls, we should pray with the psalm writer. Psalm 19:12-13. We all have hidden faults that we do not confess. Whispering our sin to God is good. God offers another thing. James 5:16.

Only unforgiven sin can damn our souls. If Christ has covered all our sin, and if God imputes to us the perfect righteousness of Christ, the case against us fails. Romans 8:33-34.

Longsuffering is fierce as the Apostle Paul wrote to Timothy. II Timothy 2:24-26. We can not afford to be self-absorbed. Our life pattern can transform us into a watered garden that will lift the gloom and turn it into light that brings us through the rest of our journey.

Joy overflows or it dies. Matthew 10:32-33. God is longsuffering and willing to forgive us. Little by little a life can be built on grace and forgiveness that comes from God.

"Forgiveness is the beginning of the cleansing of the soul."

John Calvin

Chapter Four
Longsuffering as a Sacred Journey

Longsuffering is the reality of daily life. Suffering is woven into our lives. Longsuffering is a healing journey. The destination is joy. Paths in life are cut short by accidents, broken limbs, stolen wallets, or death of a loved one. None of us escapes the hurts and pains. Matthew 5:45.

The Bible gives serious warnings about apostasy. False prophets arise. Love will grow cold Those who endure to the end will be saved. Matthew 24:11-13. Paul said many disciples will be drawn away. Acts 20:29-30. The warnings are important to those called by the Spirit.

Faithfulness and diligence explains the many warnings against apostasy in the Holy Scriptures. The Word of God is an instrument used by the Spirit for our sanctification. Paul shares his own need for confidence in the preservation of God. II Timothy 4:18.

Remaining preserved involves personal responsibility and keeping ourselves in the love of God. On the basis of faith, our longsuffering preserves us through Jesus the Christ. Jude 3.

Our sacred journey will still be in progress as we are mindful of what grace teaches us to deny ungodliness and worldly lusts. We will encounter stealthy people. We are immune from infiltration. The grace-filled path seeks and loves God. On our spiritual journey, we will view a world drowning in sin. God will still be in charge.

Longsuffering needs not to destroy us. It actually has the potential for abundant life. Scripture teaches us through Paul that as we "groan inwardly, we wait eagerly for healing and transformation. Romans 8:23.

Many will carry deep hurts because human beings inflict longsuffering on each other. Evil means for our suffering will destroy us, but God means suffering for good.

Consciousness and Spirituality

There are states of awareness that comes on our sacred journey.

Spirituality is related to consciousness. Love eventually produce a mature growth in consciousness. Humans have potentials The Holy Spirit will lead us to where we are needed. God exists in a realm transcendent to what our senses perceive. God only loves. Our pains and sufferings do not negate that love. Love is fulfilling. Christ is here to support us.

We all hate suffering, especially as our body weakens and brings unexpected hurts with wear and tear on our bodies. As we get older, we find nothing helps. God wants us to consider the path of suffering is a sacred journey. I Peter 2:21. Some illnesses do not succumb with medical help.

Most of us tend to believe we have done something wrong. Dr. James Riley told my wife that she had breast cancer, he said wisely, "This is not your fault." The journey has the potential to heal or to harm. We have all heard the phrase, "Life is difficult, and then we die."

There is something wrong with everything in our imperfect world. So people get entrenched in their negative stance toward life. On most airplane crashes, some survive. A reporter asked a woman, "Were you afraid?" The survivor answered, "I knew it was my time to go, then fine. If it was not my time, I would just relax."

She suffered for years from the injuries to her body. She worked toward healing, not fatalism. She knew her suffering was inevitable. Her faith insured that God was in control. Fatalism is morally lazy. This view has no imagination or dream. We are not the masters of our destinies.

God lets trouble come to good people. We ask, "Why do bad things happen to good people?" We are frail human beings. One result of suffering is that we think the world is collapsing around us. Pain brings people face to face with reality. When we experience troubles, we realize how great God is. Psalm 103:15-17.

God wants a life of faith, not just a few bursts of faith. God desires that people cope with the hard grind of daily life. Our troubles are not unique. It may come to me in differing ways. We are never prepare for them. You are not a special target for the worst blows.

Our roots are not deep enough.

We lapse and fall during the storms of life because our roots are not deep enough. Longsuffering brings deep roots. The deeper the rootage, the greater our lifting power when the time comes for us to raise a great burden that we did not choose.

When we move through the valley of suffering, sorrow, and disappointment, we need to be quiet, trust in God's goodness. Wait. Do nothing rashly or quickly. March forward believing that all things will work together for good.

Our roots insure our sense of God becomes more explicit and personal trough faith and prayer. All good spiritual ideas, preconceptions, and projections are encountered in the silence.

In prayer, we remember that we are entirely committed ad dependent on God. God is an undefinable mystery. A stream of water knows where it is going. The raft of Christ will hold us. Stay on board.

Love flowers beautifully in the good soil, in the roots that run deep. God's deep roots are filled with love.

Energy for Positive Living

The story is told of a Nebraska farmer who found a baby eagle in one of his fields. The poor young eaglet was not in good condition. The farmer took it into his home to nurture it. Over the next few weeks, the bird was getting better. The farmer placed it in with his chicks. In a few days, the eagle became listless. The farmer thought the eagle was going to die.

He put the eagle in his pickup truck. He headed across the border into Wyoming when he found a family of eagles. He let the eagle fly free. It spread its wings as new energy surged into his body.

An incredible source of energy is available to us. That unlimited energy source makes a difference in our lives. We have been designed for more than ever could be imagined.

Human beings are limited. Our bodies are not designed to run forever. Unlimited and eternal describes God.

If we are to grow physically, we need to take in nourishment. Our intellectual, emotional, and spiritual lives need the same. We need nourishment and encouragement from God.

The Bible speaks to us about the strength, power, and energy available to us. Psalm 68:35, Ephesians 6:10, Philippians 4:13, and Romans 15:13. We might repeat three affirmations in our time with God. I am created in the image of God. I am essentially a spiritual being. I am created for a relationship with God.

Coach Guy B. Crawford brought his Dobyns-Bennet Indians basketball team to Bristol's Tennessee High's then cracker box size gymnasium in February 1958.

Destined to be the best team in their history, they had won 36 games and lost only two. The Indians had battered the Tennessee Vikings 90-33 in the first game played in January.

The thin Vikings didn't have a player more than six feet tall. The Tennessee High coach reminded them that if they tried to run with them, they would grow weary, if we walk, we faint not. Miraculously, the game was tied after the first half. It stayed tied at the end of the regulation time.

In overtime, Dobyns-Bennet led 39-38 with seconds on the clock. The Kingsport team had the ball. A Viking stole the ball and raced in for a lay- up. The ball rimmed over the orange steel circle, and the struggling Vikings lost again.

To this day Bristol fans say, "What if?"

Do not run with this world that is so out of control. Walk with God as you renew your strength. You will soar like the eagle. One day you will run and not grow weary.

Hoping for the Joys of Heaven

The hope of heaven makes life and death much easier. Sadly, some expressed no hope of heaven. The hope-filled say they are closer to seeing glory. Longsuffering ends with a foretaste of heaven. We talk about heaven, but those dying are actually making the transition. They believe their last breath will take them to the presence of God. Human history reveals that people have always sought a promise of heaven.

From the beginning of time, people want to hold faith the idea of going to a better place. Revelation 21:4. Paul expressed it well in his letter to Philippi. Philippians 1:22-24. Were created for heaven, and we will be restless until we get there.

Death appears to be the most final, unavoidable fact of life. Everybody dies. Hoping for the joys of heaven permits us to turn our thoughts toward heaven. We can see the big picture.

Awakening to the Spirit-led Journey

The awakening of ourselves to the Holy Spirit within our personal encounters and experiences. In this sacred moving in the Spirit, we respond to the internal direction. Most spiritual writers assume the reader has already been filled with the Spirit. We will be reading in the context of the entire spiritual path. Spirituality is responding to the Spirit. I have been led by Christ to understand my goal in Christian spirituality that meets my needs as a highly sensitive introvert within grace to respond to the movement of the Spirit.

The completion of our salvation occurred on Pentecost with the sending of the Holy Spirit to the Christian church community. The Holy Spirit is the energy of the community's life together and the life of each individual who has joined the community. The Spirit initiates our sanctification. Galatians 5:25. I came to understand that the external performance of good deeds was only as good as the internal love that was my motivation. Simultaneously I felt a freedom to let go of some external performances that did not help my sacred journey. II Corinthians 3:17.

Many Christians put their focus of their spiritual lives on getting to know the Jesus from Scripture. They then imitate the example of Christ. Another focus is to be faithful to the will of God. The prayer energy is for doing the will. This was the focus of Jesus' own goals. Other Christians are awakened by loving and serving others. They concentrate their effort on being faithful in helping others in need.

Each of these approaches are valid. Each one is supported by plenty of references in the New Testament. Each complements the others. Spirit is crucial in any imitation of Jesus. I Corinthians 12:3.

The Bible teaches that we cannot recognize Jesus as Lord without the Spirit. The same Holy Spirit that I received at my own conversion is the same that moved in Jesus' life. Jesus was conceived, baptized, and led by the Spirit. The Spirit was sent to me by the Father God. Romans 8:15-16.

Therefore, the Spirit I received is the Spirit of God. God is love. We are able then to love God and neighbor. The more I am open to God inside of me and I open to love all those I may encounter. I John 4:7-8.

The apostle Paul says as much. Galatians 5:16-23. Christ's death freed us from the consequences of sin. The grace placed inside us is stronger than the sin within us, so we can trust our deeper redeemed self. Romans 8:12-

13. The sacred transition in the life of Paul gave him and us a new freedom. II Corinthians 3:17. Only after we have experienced the awakening of the Holy Spirit can we respond to the Spirit. Faithfulness in responding will bring us into deeper and deeper with Jesus and God.

The awakening could happen in an effort to cope with negative and life- threatening encounters such as the breaking up of a relationship we may have cherished, career frustration, failure, death of our loved one, and theological concerns.

Our continuing conversion is our spiritual path. If we remain faithful to the guidance of the Spirit in our ordinary daily life, we trust the Spirit to lead us to the most intimate joining to Christ and God's people. Jesus is no longer jus an acquaintance about whom we heard from others. Christ is now our personal friend. We now have a deeper desire to know Jesus, to know and serve him. We find ourselves wanting to spend more time with him.

Our continuing conversion occurs in our external actions. In some areas of our life, we are doing well. The habits of sin are receding, but in other areas, we might not be doing as well. The Holy Spirit gets us more in tune with ourselves. Consequently my writing is done more and more under the guidance of the Spirit. I find myself writing feelings and insights that I have not previously reflected on. I relax with a cup of green tea as I write. I must not get myself into a rush. I pause in prayer before I write anything.

Proverbs 5 gives us wisdom on the temptations we face. This passage gives insight into temptation. The best defense against sexual temptation is healthy and joy-filled marriage. Our choices bring blessings or if we choose wrongly, it has negative unrighteous consequences. The fifth chapter of Proverbs brings two women before us. We are introduced to the adulteress. Proverbs 5:3. The writer also speaks of "the wife of your youth." Proverbs 5:18. The world asks questions about feelings associated with a relationship. The Scripture draws a circle around any relationship. The Bible is clear on what is appropriate.

Proverbs instructs us in the first words of the chapter, "Her lips are like honey." There is an initial sweetness about her. Her speech is smoother than oil. We are not aware that her sweetness will turn to wormwood. The end of the dangerous encounter is not like the beginning.

In the beginning her ways are unstable and she is not aware. We should have compassion for her. Of course, Proverbs could have written about an ignorant him.

Look at the end of the story. People who are seduced away from their spouse and abandon their children find their own lives slipping away. Modern divorce courts foster antagonism that grows and grows. Lawyers might stretch a divorce out and it costs everyone lots of money. Everybody loses. The children have less time with their parents. Someone else ends up raising your children.

Verse 11 discusses the wasting away of the body. This reference might refer to sexually transmitted diseases. You will groan in the end when your body and flesh are consumed. It was common then and common today. All bodies age and become weaker. The fires of the temptation do not last forever. Verses 12-13 is about self-recrimination. You will be angry at yourself for what you have done.

The fire of sexual love.

The fire of sexual love is outside the fireplace of a lifetime commitment. A few minutes of being warmed by the fire of sex are not worth years of getting burned, and the guilt and shame are high prices to pay. The fire of sex is powerful. Sexuality is a gift from God to warm us where it burns in the fireplace of married love.

You did not "rejoice in the wife of your youth." The physical relationship includes the reality that the bald spots and wrinkles start to show. Gray hair and stretch marks show on every woman. The wife of your youth was the one you married. You grew together and produced children. Remember her in the early days, in the middle days, and the later days. Enjoy the history that you made together. She was longsuffering. She stood beside you through every experience. Some of your history involved difficult things. Some was painful, some wonderful. The adulteress will never share those days with you.

Your chosen wife or husband cultivates eternal love and joy. Marriage involves making love with the one you walked with, slept wit, talked with, sensibly and freely. The potential for joy, for ecstasy, for delight, and for refreshment comes with faithful marriage. The promises of seduction will not come to pass. There will be utter bitterness.

God delights in married love. The Lord distains unrighteous expressions. Renewal of your eternal love will bring the joy of intimacy.

Names are safe and anonymous.

I am careful not to mention the names of others with whom I have encountered. I write what emerges in my soul in the quietness. I never have a pre-conceived format about what might be included in a particular book.

Sensitive writers often over-react and try to discern whether the Spirit is or is not present. When I do not feel the Spirit, I fail to sense the full emergence of what is welling up from the center of my being.

The spiritual journey is the sacred road to freedom. The goal of our life on earth is to love God and others with our whole heart, soul, mind, and body. As we move closer each day toward the realization that we really are more free and loving.

We are becoming what we were created to be. That freedom comes from living in tune with the Holy Spirit. II Corinthians 3:17. Nothing can come between our response to the presence of God as we enjoy being more loving and full of grace.

Progress in Faith

There will continue to be areas will need to grow. Our spiritual journey involves setting right what has gone wrong. We make progress in fellowship and love. We build a personal relationship. God came down in Jesus to be intimate with us as our gracious, forgiving, and loving Father.

Love, grace, and joy cannot be carried to excess. Agape love is love initiated by the Lover with burning desire to love. God's love is active. It is not mere sentiment cherished in the soul. It is primarily an attitude toward another that moves us and God to act n meeting the needs of the one that is loved.

The apostles of Jesus made the connection between the truth about our future destiny impacting our present part of our journey. We will make healthy progress in or faith including joy and thanksgiving, fellowship, and holiness. Seek the Lord's grace and strength. Jude 24.

One of God's goals is experiential sanctification which means to change into the character of Jesus. Our progress in faith includes the stabilized inner life. Our inner motives and desires become pure and blameless.

Spiritual progress depends upon an increasing awareness of our dependence on God. We are not in charge of our circumstances. If love is absent, there will be less faithfulness. I John 2:6.

Walking consists of two steps repeated over and over and over again. In the same way our spiritual journey requires two steps, one step after another. The spiritual journey is not one of mediocrity. We are to keep walking toward excellence. God desires that we move beyond the status quo.

As we sang in summer vacation Bible school," Every day with Jesus is sweeter than the day before." This is the simple aspect of sanctification. Sanctification is what we set our minds to. Don't let the mind wander off. The Spirit will keep us on target. II Corinthians 10:3-5.

Challenge to Strive for Excellence

Jesus told us that anybody can learn to love people who love them. Anyone can be kind to people who are kind in turn. That is easy. Christ's followers strive for love for people who have nothing in common with us. God teaches us to love each other.

The Christian journey is a walk that does not bring attention to itself but focuses on Christ. The world promotes ungodly ambition. Earthly interests have less importance. Excellence is the gradual result of striving to do better. The challenge is to be persistent. The essence of excellence is that it is accomplished in conscious reliance on God.

The challenge is to build a bridge for the gospel. Love is the measuring rod for character. A summary of the challenge for excellence is that love must be our motive behind everything we do which is encouraging, exhorting, teaching, helping, comforting. We progress more and more in stimulating love by modeling love.

We model love

The God of all comfort sent Christ Jesus and we are comforted. With the Holy Spirit, e comfort one another with a loving touch, by our presence, by our empathy, and reenforcing our faith with conviction and passion.

Those who do marathons and iron man running get aching legs, burning throats, and an urge to stop. Friends and fans who have journeyed far to see you race helps to push through the pain on to the finish line. We are accountable to God and to those whom we have encountered in our earthy journey.

God is in the soul and our soul is in God. God is always in the soul to give it life, to love it, and to try to lead it. To our days of longsuffering, the soul is drawn into the deeper realms of silence. He sacred soul becomes increasingly free to follow the guidance of the Spirit.

This the fruit of our spiritual journey and that is why God created us. (Philip Saint Romain, *The Logic of Happiness*, p.70) When the water in a pond is calm, dirt settles, and we can see the bottom, God's glory shines within us.

The spirit speaks to us and consoles us in our pain and suffering. Pray for grace to be healed. Feel loved despite the pain. Pray the Serenity Prayer. Romans 8:18. There is the principle of synchronicity. We are drawn to encounter people, circumstances, books, and things that deepen our lives. Matthew 6:33.

Mutual Responsibilities to One Another

God created us to serve. Continue to function. Admonish those who are idle. Encourage the faint-hearted and the discouraged. We must help hose who are morally, physically, and spiritually weak.

Be patient with one another It is never easy to deal with people. Overcome evil with good actions. Don't curse them, bless them. Pray for them. We at some point on the journey will experience the revelation that we are imperfect Christians.

Love suffers long. We must bear each other's worst behavior. Love is kind. Our spiritual journey includes seeking ways to be useful in other people's lives. Never delight in another's unrighteous acts nor join in the expression. We must be silent toward one another's faults. Love bears all things. Express your unshakeable confidence in faithfulness. Love endures all things. Longsuffering includes praying without ceasing. The essence of intimate prayer is dependence that is woven into the heart of faith. Pray repeatedly and often. We rejoice in appreciation for the righteous character of God. We are grateful for the ministry of the Holy Spirit. We rejoice in the providence of God working for us. It is difficult to distinguish between spirit and soul. In salvation faith includes the renewing of both.

This renewal includes building each other up. Living in peace. Warning the idle. Encouraging the timid. Helping the weak. Being patient. Being joyful. Giving thanks. Stirring up the Spirit's fire within us and counting on God's help. Renewal is the anticipation of complete sanctification.

The world sees self-image is a factor. The sacred path of a believer is positive, other people will appear good, inviting, and exciting. If our self- image is negative, the world appears angry, hostile, fearful creating difficulty in understanding the relationships with others. They walk a way that views the world as pessimistic living, building themselves up and tearing others down.

Believers conclude that those lost on the wrong pathway have a narcissist personality. A psychotherapist would say they have an excessive self- importance. They crave attention. They are skilled in the art of deception. They will not just disappear quietly.

Others demonstrate a paranoid personality with delusions of grandeur, hypernasality, and are always looking for ulterior motives. They experience little guilt or anxiety over the pain they inflict on others.

This transformation is based on the faithfulness of God and the soverentity of God. We will then communicate the truth and grow in grace. Sanctification is the door into communion with God. The desire of God for our lives is to be progressively more set apart. God makes even more difference in our lives in the present than yesterday.

Jesus will make more and more difference on our spiritual path. With greater awareness of Presence, our behavior will be impacted. We are not to shrink back from total commitment to the will of God even though it involves longsuffering.

Accept the suffering from the lens of eternity and in the context of commendable conduct. The worst the world can do to us is to kill us as they did Jesus. We will possess submissiveness and patience and the mind of Christ. A proper mind-set dedicates ourselves to the will of God.

We know that we have a limited time to produce. I Peter 1:13. We are to guide the sheep, protect the sheep with discernment, discipline the sheep. and know the sheep, care about them, and spend time with them is the summary of what Jesus said to Peter at a post-resurrection breakfast.

This encounter with Peter shows our need to take personal responsibility. Jesus taught that keeping the commandments is the foundation to abiding in the love of God.

This is how we are loved by the Father. John 14:21,23. This is how we are loved by Jesus. John 15:9-10. Look for the mercy of God. Eternal life is not earned, but it is given to us in Christ. We must be compassionate. This is more important now than it has ever been. On your life journey, build your faith. II Peter 1:5-7. Pray in the Holy Spirit. Romans 8:26. Keep yourselves in the love of God. John 15:9.

An ounce of prevention is worth a pound of cure. Pray according to the leading of the Spirit. Keep abiding in the love of God. Walk with God. Stay committed.

Remember our walk with God is a sacred journey.

"Step by step, a sacred journey.

Birth is a beginning and death a destination." Karen Levi

Chapter Five
Longsuffering People Focus on Jesus

Jesus told his disciples, "Follow me, and I will make you fishers of men." Walking in faith is to focus on Jesus. Faithfulness includes risk, danger, difficulties with potential for discouragement.

Even his close disciples lived with the temptation to quit. The character of faith presses on and continues. The finish line is our time of death which brings us into the kingdom of God. Finishing the race is more important than starting the race.

Shocking his disciples, Jesus taught them how much faith is needed. Luke 17:1-6. Another shock was his rapid turn to forgive, once there is repentance. Uprooting trees and planting them in the sea is a way to view salvation.

Jesus breaks down our schemes of life. Our views about right and wrong Our faith is small, that is Faith is a childlike wonder so filled with goodness, it is hard to believe. Jesus says that we forgive on the basis of knowing I am forgiven.

Blessed means full of joy. Matthew 5:4. Paul describes longsuffering faithfulness as momentary. II Corinthians 4:16-18. To see with the eyes of faith that which is not in the present now and one day will be even better.

It is easy to become spiritually weary if we are not prepared by the Holy Spirit for the obstacles and length of our time on earth. Keep running the race. Hebrews 12:1-3. The writer of Hebrews points to the character of witnesses who have proven by their testimony that they were faithful in their journeys.

Noah patiently labored before the devastation of the flood for 120 years. Noah is an example of longsuffering.

Abraham left the comfort of his hometown Ur and walked an unfamiliar path that was uncomfortable.

We are all designed so that some particular sin, a particular struggle, an alluring temptation that is difficult to overcome. Take the concept and fruit of love. Some distort it into temptations that can destroy us little by little. People become objects of our focus. We can't stop thinking about that person. Erotic love allows for no resistance. We expose our deepest vulnerabilities with no illusions to self-mastery. The seducer tells us tat nobody is capable of loving us like they can. Love gets us off center. The potential lover becomes more vivid than any other encounter. So we surrender to their love without counting the cost. This love feeds on hundreds of feelings that both have never experienced in their lives.

Love is a realm beyond that opens spiritual awareness. He or she might say, "If you ever leave me, it will cost you." Private love is made public. Both are now forever on edge. Loving always involves two highly sensitive souls who act out of proportion and they will overreact or overthink the mystery.

Life's race is described as an agony. Life is never easy. Each experience is not a bed of roses. There are no warnings or expectations. Amos 6:1. Our strength is not in ourselves, but in the Holy Spirit.

Our life encounters and journeys are personal. So we forgive and are forgiven as we keep focusing on Jesus. Jesus fuels our faithfulness. Jesus has already blazed the trail for us.

So Jesus is the unshakable ground for us. Jesus anticipates our joy. David Brooks concludes his book in these words: "Joy is not produced because others praise you. Joy emanates unbidden and unforced. Joy comes as a gift when you least expect it. At those fleeting moments you know why you were put here and what truth you serve. You may not feel giddy at those moments. You may not hear the orchestra's delicious swell or see flashes of crimson and gold, but you will feel a satisfaction, a silence, a peace—a hush. Those moments are blessings and the signs of a beautiful life." David Brooks, *The Road to Character*, p. 270.

Jesus will show us how to be found faithful. Paul tells that that he glories in his weakness. Our human encounters were difficult, but not too difficult for Jesus.

Life's encounters attack us, especially through people who have the capacity to hurt us emotionally, physically, and spiritually. We are constantly being discouraged. To have a mountain be cast into the sea, we are to identify what it is. Past negative experiences can keep us in bondage. Finances can bring struggles into a marriage or relationship to create unnecessary stress. Physical illness, emotional suffering, or poor thinking quenches the fire of our faith. Calling our mountains by name recognizes the cause of our longsuffering.

To understand mountain moving faith, Jesus asks us to consider the mustard seed. The mustard seed illustrates powerful potential not just small size faith. The mustard seed illustrates our limitation. Jesus said the Word of God is like a seed. The power of God displays the glory of God. Mustard seed faith illustrates expectation. We are limited in viewing the seed making the transformation. Hebrews 11:1. A seed requires time and growth to break through the soil.

All the bad things that have happened in our lives are not the result of our lack of faith. Life happens, but we must keep on in faith and enjoy the gifts of the Holy Spirit.

Being more like Jesus brings more than anyone could anticipate. He was so unpredictable. He was playful, intense, and confusing. The goal of our redemption is to become human. Jesus was fully human and fully God. Redeemed people live with imagination and joy. Jeremiah 17:9.

Jesus was deeply intrigued by humans. Review the story of his encounter with the woman at the well. John 4. Being willing to risk and encounter others. Luke 17:20-21. He saw what is impossible to see. Fix your eyes on Jesus. II Corinthians 4:18. Spiritual imagination moves our glimpse to see what life was meant to be.

Most people desire predictable lives. Predictability is ordered time and space. The Holy Spirit reminds us with a spirited hunger for what we will become. Jesus life was quite radical as it drew others to God.

Becoming more fully human is to be like Jesus. Each person does it differently, in her unique way. We are to bring glory to God. Hebrews 13:15-16. Our faithfulness brings delight to God.

The Spirit calls each of us to live as a unique human in this particular world with specific people. The fruit of the Spirit enforces our gifts. This fruit are supernatural endowments. Every moment we become entangled in somebody else's story. Every encounter has the potential to change our lives. Surprising encounters are expected. Moving from the future to the present challenges us to change and face what keeps us from loving and being loved by Christ.

We will begin to realize both the foolishness of our sin and the beauty of Christ's loving heart. The joy of an involvement with another is greater than the risk of being rebuffed. People in longsuffering pain need to talk.

Every encounter that I ever experienced has oozed out forgiveness. Love is forever. Love never stops. Focus on Jesus during these longsuffering times.

Praying s opening our consciousness to a loving relationship with God. Spending time alone with God, the one who loves us best. Offer your prayer time to God. Ask the Spirit and be aware of your guardian angel to lead.

Eternity rushes before us.

It arrives like a speeding meteor that will one day hit this earth. Live in light of the eternity streaking toward us. When we interact with others, God moves among and through us.

These encounters enrich our human bond. When we refuse to interact with others, you block the flow of God in the human community. God flows through creation.

Jesus Is the Source of Our Joy

God-given joy is the fruit of the Spirit. We need not fear losing joy. Joy remains constant and consistent regardless of our circumstances. The joy of the Lord is our personal strength flowing from the love and grace of God.

I came to realize that joy is a permanent gift. Our joy is always present. Joy remains constant in our difficult encounters. I enjoy visiting the Great Smokey Mountains. I love those hazy mountains. In the evening, darkness keeps them from my view, but I know they are still there.

Just as the beautiful mountains in Tennessee and North Carolina remain steadfast and firm even in the darkness. The joy of Jesus in you makes our joy forever full. Jesus is our source of joy. Joy is permanent, powerful, personal and present. I Peter 1:8. Remember these words while you live in the Spirit and with the gift of longsuffering.

Be passionate for Jesus. As long as e pile on the wood and draw close to God, the wind of the Holy Spirit will fan the flames. The fire must be so hot that even a rainstorm of adversity will not douse the flame. The fire will smolder. Longsuffering gives us more insight than we can ever imagine.

If you only knew that abiding in Christ Jesus. We all bear some measures of fruit. We are connected with Christ. Christ said he was the true vine. We are abiding or not abiding. Some people have an external connection to he kingdom, but they are not part of it. Matthew 7:15-23, Romans 11:13-24.

The fruit of the Spirit gives evidence that we are children of God. Matthew 3 and Matthew 7. The fruit is being like Jesus. There are differing levels of fruit bearing. We are to bear as much fruit as we can. The ultimate goal is bring glory to God.

Fruit bearing is the purpose of our lives. If you only know the possibilities of our potential to become like Jesus. Longsuffering is the pruning knife of God.

We use the phrase "going home to be with God." Home is where we bring our friends. Home is where our hearts are and where we desire to be. Home is our place of safety and security. Home is the place where we feel comfortable. Home is the base for our work, the center of what we do. Home is where we find strength for life. Home is our abiding place.

We sing, "The world is not my home, I'm just passing through." Persecuting becomes more palatable. We are not to imagine that our longsuffering is unique. We do not avoid persecution by conforming with the world. John 15:19.

Persecution is not your fault. Hatred is never excused. The Holy Spirit is the witness for the truth. John 15:26-27. We cannot handle life by ourselves. Jesus wants us to understand the world's hatred toward his followers. Abiding in Christ is the source for our own life journey.

Living in the light exposes the darkness. Our ethics expose the duplicity of the world's methods. The world's behaviors are condemned by God. Our compassion exposes the insensitive and self-absorption of the world. To be like Jesus we must be united together by the bonds of affection because the world, our common enemy, hates us.

If then the purest love which was ever witnessed, if goodness incarnate was held, if the brighter Jesus' love is shone, the harder will be the response. If you only knew the Holy Spirit as an expansion of the ministry of Jesus. John 16:7.

Jesus could not physical be everywhere geographically at one time or place, but the Holy Spirit can be anywhere. Jesus spoke of progressive revelation. John 16:12. He taught a purposeful revelation. John 16:13. He told of prophetic revelation. John 16b. He also gave the insights of particular revelation. John 16:14-15. The Holy Spirit's ministry is Jesus Christ centered.

The Holy Spirit convicts the world of sin, all of us believers have a part to play. The Spirit focus is on Jesus. The Spirit will break down the indifference of the typical pagan unbeliever who has no conviction of sin. Jesus is behind all things. He is the Lord of life.

How can we understand that this man with a dated history, is at one and the same God. He showed greatness, sovereignty, and profundity, and he was called God. Jesus being God is a scandal to the Jewish people and to religious and pious people of yesterday and today. Jesus is a God, a totally other beyond his world, who cannot be objectified, eternal, infinite, incomprehensible, above everything human beings are. We Christians find that the God of the Jew became concrete as a man, Jesus of Nazareth.

Seeing, imitating, and deciphering Jesus, by living together with him, we come to know God. Our God who reveals eternal divineness in Jesus, the human being.

God communicates to us through a Son.

Jesus being God is significate. God speaks in a Son. He speaks in our language and shows us his secret beauty in our world.

Seeing Jesus by faith connects us to joy. The joy of the Lord is our strength. Seek clarification from Jesus, only he can move the fog of confusion. John 16:19. Jesus knows our every need even before we ask. Focus on the right questions. John 16:20-22.

The lasting nature of joy proves that it exists through the entire dispensation of the Spirit, not just in the time right after the resurrection. Faith transacts requests into the joy of the good gifts from God. Joy comes from asking and receiving. John 16:24. Love is the fruit that meets our needs. Jesus, God, and the Holy Spirit have an eternal co-existence.

The joy of the disciples after the resurrection of Jesus will be the joy of a new life in which their relations with God will be more direct and more confident. There is now more comfort for painful times. They shall have the guidance of God in uncertain times. They can enjoy God's fellowship in any time. In impossible times they have the power of God.

"Healing in this life is not resolution of the past.

It is using our past to draw us into a deeper relationship with Jesus and his unique purpose for our lives."

Dan Allender

Chapter Six
Longsuffering and Character

Suffering opens ancient places of pain that has been hidden. Our own limitations are revealed through longsuffering. Suffering, like love, shatters the illusion of self-mastery. Longsuffering is a reminder of human finitude. It pushes us to see life in its widest connections, which is where character is found.

Heraclitus reminded us long ago about developing good character. The ancient philosopher wrote: "Good character is not formed in a week or a month. It is created little by little, day by day. Patient effort is needed to develop good character."

President Abraham Lincoln said, "Character is like a tree. reputation is like its shadow. The shadow is what we think, the tree is the real thing." Every experience and each encounter contributes to the person we have become today.

Imitating the character of God we care deeply. Character brings our memories and work and faithfulness into God's eternal joy. We too weep when one of our fellow ministers die. We will no longer see their face in this world. Pressing on toward the goal is the only way to run the race of being like Jesus in character. Character means pressing on. It is the foundation for running the race. Character is a work ethic of diligence. Character helps us persevere.

Put on Longsuffering

Growing within us are the fruits of the Spirit. The ability to endure and to forgive is an active decision for us. You can put on the nature of Jesus. That shows that you have chosen Christ. Galatians 3:27.

Our weaknesses, unwillingness, and our failures need not push us down. Be open about he failures so others have the pathway to freedom despite our sins.

Those without character show a lack of contentment, complaining, grumbling, indifference, and ungratefulness. Longsuffering builds strong character. It is sanctified suffering. Television preacher Joyce Meyer said, "Patience is not simply the ability to wait. Patience is how we behave while we are waiting."

What if you went into a large city to buy groceries. You drive into the parking lot. As you remove your seat belt and unlock your door, you look down to see if your car is within the yellow lanes. As you look down, you notice a wallet on the ground. You pick it up and notice it is heavier than your wallet. It is loaded with green money with more than one zero on it. There is no identification in the wallet. There is no one around that saw you pick up this loaded wallet. You begin to think that this crisp abundance of bills will pay off many of your debts. I could get my car repaired. I could pay another month on my house loan.

But then the Spirit speaks to you. This is not your wallet. This is not your money. It belongs to some other person. There was no identification. Your have a choice. You could just keep the wallet and the money. The world has declared, "Finders keeps, losers weepers."

Another choice would be just to leave the wallet there, not get involved. You go on your way. You could take the wallet into the grocery store to ask if anybody has asked about a lost wallet. If no one knows anything about it, you might write up a "found" article. Put a note in the classifieds. You did not steal money or rob a bank. You merely picked up trash that somebody left on the ground. If I just left it, it would not be my problem.

Really. Read James 4:17. One simple verse, but what a profound concept to illustrate human character.

The world's impression of sin is that it doesn't exist. Unfortunately, it is how the world looks at sin. How does a person without being filled wit the Spirit view sin. Some form the impression that obedience to God means not breaking the law. That's how the natural person thinks. I just told a lie. I just committed a small sin. They say the word "commit" quite often.

Character has a Greek origin that means "I engrave." Character is etched into us. Our goal should be consistent in dealing with others. Treat every person in the same way with grace and love. High charactered people do what they say. All nine of the fruit of the Spirit could be distorted. Peace to an evil warmonger means that they have destroyed, bombed, and made others suffer so much they give up the fight. That is their definition of peace.

Each week the sensitive leader goes over the decisions she might have made. Will your encounters reflect on you as a person of character? Strong people think about how they could have done it better.

Show humility when the world looks with envy on your achievements and success. Humility is not saying, "Pardon me for existing." Tough conversations. Prepare and decide how to engage in communication style that makes a healing difference.

We need to nurture our relationships. Spirit-filled people will eventually leave a wrong kind of relationship. Eventually, we will find a better journey on the road to character. Practice empathy when others tempt you not to be. Our strength is in the joy of the Lord. That quiet strength comes in our humiliating times.

Decide to keep up the positive things about your relationships. You will do better with other relationships. Focus on what you can do now with new encounters. That is the only way your vision and purpose can take root.

John Calvin said, "What is true character of repentance? It is not only an outward amendment of life, but its beginning is the cleansing of the heart." Paul wrote the same truth in Colossians 1:21-22. The cleaning is both outward and inward. Cleansing proves tat we have faith. Psalm 51:1-12 gives a clear picture of deep sorrow and longsuffering as we plea for forgiveness.

Building character requires longsuffering in differing ways. Examine yourself or let another do some psychotherapy or healing of your soul and what down deep you are struggling with now. If you discover it is within your self-discipline, set goals and work toward their accomplishment.

Humility is the beginning of wisdom.

Building character is not simple or easy. Humility is the beginning of wisdom. Be open to new ways of acting. Integrity is never automatic. We must be open to new ways. When we become persons of high character, takes the ability to do right over what is easy. One who becomes a master of patience is master of many things. An unbeatable combination of patience, persistence, and perspiration will build good character.

Paulo Coelho shared the purpose of longsuffering. "I have seen many storms in my lifetime. Most storms have caught me by surprise, so I had to learn quickly to look further and understand that I am not capable of controlling the weather, to exercise the art of patience and to respect the fury of nature."

People follow us because of our character. Some people may have never met you face to face, but they know of your reputation. Character is controllable. Follow through even if the situation is difficult.

We find it hard to take responsibility for our decisions. Stop searching for ways to blame others. Nobody lives a perfect life. In a United Methodist annual conference, the bishop asks if all are blameless. Actions speak louder than words. Be encouraged you can develop a new level of respect when you accept responsibility for all that happens, including your failures. When we are given God's love, grace, joy, and all the fruit of the Holy Spirit, no one is beyond redemption.

After one of my biggest failures, one of my friends sent me a card that said, "Endurance is not just the ability to bear a hard thing, but to turn it into glory." Longsuffering and endurance brings the ability to withstand hardship. Longsuffering leads to resilience. I pray that everyone involved in a hardship will recover from it and will transform the situation into glory.

To fully understand any encounter is impossible. Only God can do the impossible. I have discovered that the only safe reaction is simply to go on living, to keep on with doing your calling, and to find in Jesus Christ the strength and courage to meet life, and to know the comfort that God is afflicted in my affliction.

My own reaction to some of my failures is to be depressed. Clinical depression was all I could experience in the darkness. Longsuffering in this dark deep well, I could not eradicate the depression that was wreaking havoc on my soul. I told my friends that I did not want to go on living.

Being a highly sensitive person, my reaction to losing my visions was to exhaust myself. I knew that if I did not deal with the spiritual root of my suffering, it would be like placing a band aid on an infection. I asked God to give me the nine fruits of the Spirit, including longsuffering for my complete healing, wholeness, and restoration.

Nothing can separate us from the love of God. God dictates our destiny. Grace determines our worthiness. Our encounters and experiences can be healing tools, not just ordeals that drain joy. God tells us that in Christ, joy is unshakable even in the darkest times. John 15:11.

Negative speech drains our joy. Sinful talk is like cancer. If left unchecked and untreated, it will grow and grow until it effects the entire body. Such talk will kill the body as cancer does.

Don't go down that road. There is still time to take a successful detour. Examine yourself first before you speak. Bringing others down will never lift you up.

Be careful concerning your speech. Know how serious slander can be. Slander destroys churches and families. Take Paul's advice and encourage one another. When we are caught in a sin, make it our goal to be helpful, not hurtful. I Thessalonians 5:11.

It is worthless to befriend the world. James 4:13-17. You could die tonight. You could cross the street to retrieve your mail tomorrow and get hit by a car. Our lives are but a puff of smoke. We are like a vapor or a mist which is invisible and quickly disappears.

We do not know what tomorrow will bring into our lives. The present is the time to submit our lives to God. Today is your day to be cleaned and completely forgiven. Today is the day.

Character is Christ in you now, not merely to take you home to heaven when you die. Character is not just the result of a strong personality or a trained mind. It arises from the presence of God in the soul.

God delights to call people such as us to demonstrate life and grace. As Christians die daily, by living righteously and boldly speaking the truth of the gospel, we live out the death and life of our Lord Jesus Christ to the glory of God. Longing for the resurrection body motivates us to focus on spiritual ministry even at the cost of physical suffering. In our earthly body we groan because of the burdens of life. Romans 8:23.

We desire to be clothed in the resurrected body. Future glory inspires courage. We recognize the limits of our life journey. We walk by faith, not by sight. Our longsuffering produces genuine repentance. God's gift of endurance is a means to an end, not an end in itself. Longsuffering differs from worldly sorrow. Worldly sorrow results in separation and death. Repentance sparks deep emotion resulting in confidence, comfort, and joy.

The compassionate heart of Jesus comforts the distressed in all our circumstances. Christ responded to people who attacked him by saying, "Father, forgive them." Jesus alone brings wholeness to a broken relationship. Being yoked to unbelievers is a horrible idea. We must be yoked to our family, the Body of Christ.

Heavenly feeling are uniquely different.

In our heavenly body, we will not feel our present strain or difference, but natural. Future glory inspires our on-going commitment. Our eternal home is with Jesus. We live as pilgrims in this world. We exist in the tent of our temporary body. Our character is marked by sober living in light of the accountability we will one day face. We anticipate a body beyond imagination. It is not some kind of permanent bodiless existence. There will be no Nirvana with the peace of extinction. We will not be absorbed by God.

Eternity is not an escape into nothingness. Our new body will be a vastly superior body. In eternity there is no past or future. There is simply the present moment. God has been preparing us for something for each believer. The Bible informs us that when a faithful follower dies. Greek philosophers thought that to be a bodiless spirit was the highest level for existence. The body, to them, was a prison of the soul. They said that there was no advantage in being resurrected in another body.

Jesus approved the essential goodness of the body. He became a human body. Character with longsuffering rather than determination of our destiny is the human privilege. We are united with Christ in his death. We will be living a new life for Christ. We are to keep our eyes on eternity. We must hang in there. Early Christians had character. They endured physical sufferings: imprisonments, beatings, tumults, sleeplessness, death by stoning, burning, or crucifixion.

As our Lord of life, Jesus Christ deserves our total consecration as our starting point. Christ is the epitome of meekness and gentleness. Belonging to Christ is the privilege and security of every believer.

Character is the Christian benchmark. Followers of Christ do not have an inferior complex. There is no false humility. There is excellent knowledge. They have spiritual sense motivated by love. Christ deserves our highest faithfulness. Non-believers are enticing believers in our day away from God. We are always in danger of being led astray.

The people of God possessed spiritual character, but they always looked to the person of Jesus Christ as the ultimate role model. Simple but powerful theology is found in the children's hymn, "Jesus loved me, this I know, for the Bible tells me so." That sums up our basis for godly character.

The basis for godly character.

Patience and perseverance cannot be explained apart from the grace and love of Christ. We are empathic with the struggles others are experiencing. These struggles mirror God's deliverance. Physical weakness keeps us dependent on the grace of God. Weakness protects us from the sin of pride. Humans are always discontented. Let us see Christ and not complain. Jesus is weaving a tapestry. When Jesus is finished with it, he'll show it to us. When we see that tapestry spread out throughout eternity, we will rejoice in our resurrected body.

Helen Keller related, "We would never learn to be brave and patient, if there were only joy in the world."

Weakness is not just imperfect behaviors. Situations, circumstances wound, and experiences cause us to look weak. God does not delight in our longsuffering. The purpose of God in our weakness is to glorify Jesus the Son. A Christian serves with weakness. Our felt weakness is grounds for receiving strength from Christ to accomplish the will of God.

As ministers of the Word, Christ speaks through us. Think of spiritual leaders you have encountered that modeled the servant spirit where they have enriched you. Our character demonstrates Christ living in us. The person in whom Christ dwells will have undeniable evidence of that truth given to us. Love is the heart of our character. It includes our honesty. There are no hidden motives beneath the surface. Having character, we are prepared for any examination. We are confident because we are motivated by love and honesty.

What Is Honesty?

Honest people speak the truth. Honesty is presenting yourself in a genuine and sincere manner without any pretense and taking responsibility for feelings. Honesty involves accurately representing yourself, your intentions, and commitments.

Where does honesty appear in character strengths? Honest people are trustworthy, which contributes to honest relationships. Honesty in our relationships is being authentic and genuine. Honesty is saying what we feel and think without hiding, surprising, or manipulation. We are safe with others. Honesty is being vulnerable. It carries the risk of creating discomfort or conflict. Honesty helps people communicate.

We have to be honest with ourselves first. Honesty enables us to understand our emotions. Identify areas where we can improve. Honesty means telling the truth no matter what, even if it is uncomfortable and inconvenient. Honest people develop the skill and ability to have difficult conversations with consideration and respect.

Honesty enables authenticity. Secrets are exciting and mysterious; the truth can be freeing. Relationships deteriorate if here is no honesty. Revealing our fears and vulnerabilities feels scary, but it is important if we are to built trust.

Share how your current behaviors are cutting into a preexisting wound, which likely they are not aware of. Being honest and vulnerable helps people understand you better. Encourage others to be open and honest wit you. Honesty begets honesty and good character.

Create a safe place for sharing. Reveal your longsuffering that you are now experiencing. In the next chapter, I will share how highly sensitive people suffer.

"When the sky is the limit, roots run deep." Sandy Walker

Chapter Seven
Longsuffering and Highly Sensitive People

Less than a fourth of the population of the world are highly sensitive people. I know I am and I easily spot this trait in others. Sensitive people were born to process information deeply. Our five senses react to sounds, textures, sights, overstimulated feelings, and longsuffering. Whereas a less sensitive person would see just red as they do a jigsaw puzzle, sensitive people might see ten shades of red.

Sensitive people avoid confrontation or arguments. Sensitive souls are overwhelmed easily. Non-sensitives can be useful to leash out at anybody we have been rejected by using their insensitive power.

My grandson and I will shut down in loud, busy places such as concerts, sports events, and arguing people. Our brains are wired to process every detail deeply.

We have learned what we can ignore, what would be too much to handle. Highly sensitive people usually send compassion to an emotional encounter. We do a lot of self-monitoring and self-care. We pay close attention to detail. We need to be our own authority.

I have questioned my sensitivities. A function empowered sensitive person often shows spiritual maturity, presence, and integrity. We manage boundaries well. We recognize when to passively observe and when to witness. We can mirror another's behavior for reflection. We are comfortable with mystery. Life is not a problem to be solved, but a mystery to be lived.

Journaling and playing with language gives form to abstract experiences. Self-live, self-acceptance, and self-awareness gives us clarity, strength, and resilience.

Sensitives limit what they watch on television. They cannot stand cruelty, violence, suffering, or animal abuse as our emotional response is magnified.

When I awaken, I brew some tea and perhaps eat a yogurt or banana. I take my blood pressure, do a puzzle with my wife, building routines into my day.

When I face someone in the hallway, I am startled. Even small amounts of surprising stimulations activates my fight, flight, or freeze reactions. I shut down or make an uncharacteristic overreaction. In my history of falling in love, I fall hard and unaware of what is going on. My joy runs over. Love is wonderful and more intense, all-consuming, and beautifully overwhelming. Sensitive lovers are like emotional sponges. We find ourselves exhausted and we head to our bedroom, turn out lights, and relax.

Sensitives take on the moods of others. When they encounter someone in an angry mood, we will take on their emotions. Insensitive people make you responsible for their feelings.

When we fully experience love, we desire more.

For a highly sensitive person, a drizzle feels like a monsoon. I am an INFJ, my wife Laurel is INFP. We are the personality types who suffer more. They also love more. Sensitive people dream wider and experience deeper encounters and bliss. "The joy of the Lord is our strength." We will keep soaking in the light and spreading joy to others.

In my own experience, I am drawn to other sensitives. The have an aura of understanding and compassion. We are so highly tuned we feel emotions deeply in a complex way. They give gifts and send special cards to celebrate special occasions.

The writer of Les Misérables, Victor Hugo was a sensitive man touched by love. He wrote, "To die for lack of love is horrible." Love breathes life into the soul. Love is he only thing that brings us joy. People hop from one relationship to another and flip between their friends. The quality of our relationships determines our well-being. Love is the first fruit. Remember the line in the story, "You who suffer because you love, love still more. To die of love is to live by it."

We say that love brings pain and suffering. If we love a romantic partner and get jealous, afraid, or anxious are the real causes of pain, but not love.

Sensitive loving people suffer pain, but the cure is o love even more. Love can trigger longsuffering, but love is a healing thing. The ability to love another with all your soul brings happiness. If you love someone and they eventually hurt you, you were taught the lesson of loving and that is the most beautiful experience in the world.

Being loved is like collecting small gifts and tucking them away. Lovers have an unlimited supply of gifts to shower on one who makes you feel loved.

Sensitive types hear nearly every sound They notice every movement. Expressions on faces is processed. You do not have to an introvert to be highly sensitive. I always thought something was wrong with me. I tried to be like the majority of people. One of our traits is to cautious, going inward, and requiring time alone. Others see us as unsocial. Many note that we appear shy, timid, and weak.

We never like people to yell at us or talks down to you. We can sense moods from miles away. We might feel that this world is just too complicated.

We prefer a lower pace of life. Rushing around and doing more than is required or expected is or lot. Being a sensitive empath is a beautiful trait. We are curious about the things we do. Like Jesus, you will get weighed down by the heaviness of suffering in this world.

Sensitive people create music, poetry, art, books, or buildings that has meaning. Staying alive means creating.

Highly sensitive people tend to have stronger emotional responses than others. We notice every emotional cue. We feel emotions at least five times longer so our longsuffering has no end. We make effective counselors and therapists because we can see the details of another's soul. Being highly sensitive is a gift and a responsibility. There is absolutely nothing wrong with you. Sensitives are endowed with an important life mission and vision.

We do far more cognitive work than any other personality types. We find wonder in the smallest things. Sensitive empaths are on a spiritual journey. Life-style choices compromise our receptivity.

To be loved or admired by anyone awakens a hunger for more. It reaches down into the biggest urges of life that turns sensitive people. We cannot help to be seduced into the human fray. Every encounter in life is invited or turned away. Longsuffering results either way as we overthink the waste of squandered time. We imagine living in heaven with regret and sorrow. We can be redeemed like a desert is restored with rain. We are redeemed with the water of our tears.

Scripture teaches us that we work out our salvation with fear and trembling, with gentle patience and endurance. The apostle Paul gives the foundation of love. I Corinthians 13:4-7. Love begins with patience and it ends with perseverance. Love waits. Waiting is not passivity or inactivity. Short-term pleasure proves to not be an answer. Sensitives dream often. Dreams involve the depths of my soul's desires. Dreams are outside our control.

Love means risking life.

Love is the most profound risk of life. We must wait without time limits. Tears soften our faces. Nothing can bear fruit, take root, and flourish without our healing patience. Any love experience is an embrace, a touch of skin on skin. We surrender to the jouissance of God. Sensuality can never be separated from joy. As I often write in my books on joy, jouissance is celebrated in sensuous smell, sound, sight, touch, and taste.

God is love. Remember your encounters with love for those fleeting tastes are incredibly sweet. God was there. God waits for us and runs toward us. Love looks for us and as we return to our Lord hat will eventually be even more joy. Nothing is as comprehensible as God being present in every situation and encounter in all the days of our lives. All the days. The evangelist D. L. Moody said, "A faith that fizzles before it finishes had a fatal flaw from the first."

The love and grace of God give us a special freedom. It is a mystery to be lived. Our losses are insufferable. Philippians 2:5-8. Love does not grasp and hold on to other people compelling them to live for us. Every person we encounter is a being we are meant to bless. The intertwining of souls nourishes and grows, giving courage to walk on further in the longsuffering healing journey.

All human relationships change due to transitions, death, or separation breaks the continuity. The reality of all these changes keeps us from investing deeply and wildly in other people. Longsuffering takes a lifetime for sensitive people. I pray that each person I have ever encountered on earth will fill their clock time with joyous anticipation. Joy is not the absence of struggle or sorrow whatever our life story may contain. Certainly our past shapes our future. Focus on the present not on your longsuffering past. We can seize the present with insight and vision. We will encounter new relationships. We will develop new goals. Keep walking the new path, and we will experience the most profound characteristic of eternal joy.

Many people go through life wondering about their salvation. They are not sensitive to the mystery of forgiveness. "Nothing in our hands we bring, only to the cross we cling." The Titanic received six warnings about icebergs and was encouraged to change course. They ignored the warnings.

If we are willing to change course when warned by God, we will avoid disaster and enjoy the voyage of life. It is easy to drift with the current. It is difficult to return against the stream. We must consider our focus on Jesus. Hebrews 3:1. Jesus removed our sin. We were made holy, sanctified by him. We are given a new way of looking at ourselves. Jesus calls us his brothers and sisters. Jesus enables us to complete our heavenly callings.

The writer of the book of Hebrews called Jesus "the apostle and high priest of our confession." Hebrews 3:6. An apostle is an envoy, one who has sent a message. God's final word was spoken in Jesus. Focus on Jesus to bring us salvation. He first communicated the gospel and he embodied it. Write down your thoughts about Jesus. Writing, as opposed to merely thinking, assures our focus as we find that Jesus is faithful. Hebrew 3:2-6. The glory and honor that Jesus is worthy of comes from his faithfulness.

During our awareness of Jesus, we need sincere focus. Jesus is faithful. The Bible encourages us to see for ourselves. There is a lot of incentive to do this. We know enough about who Jesus is and what he has done for us, so we look further, harder, and deeper. As Philip told Nathaniel, "Come and see."

It is not easy to keep going steadily against ridicule and resistance. We are tempted to lose heart. In Jesus there is unrelenting pressure from without, but Jesus is with us to withstand and overcome. Luke 18:1. (Sarah Hornsby, *Ibid.*, p. 258)

The profession of our faith insures our becoming holy brothers with a heavenly calling. Every provision of God for the Christian believer is found in Christ. We cling to acceptance in the beloved. Ephesians 1:6. We are made into the righteousness of God. II Corinthians 5:21. We are spiritually complete in Jesus. Colossians 2:10.

We confess that Jesus Christ alone can save us. We are partakers of Christ every day. We expect the power of Jesus to inspire our faith. The Holy Spirit were inspired by the Holy Spirit. Psalm 95. The Holy Spirit continues to speak trough Scripture. Life looked completely bleak. Sometimes it seems to us that the Lord has led us into a dangerous encounter where our hopes and dreams and desires wane and break lose.

Back in the year 1956, C.S. Lewis, a confirmed bachelor, married Joy Davidman. After four happy years, Joy died. Lewis was alone again. He entered a time of longsuffering in a crisis of faith. Lewis read Hebrews 3:12-19.

When we are faced with discouraging circumstances that appear to contradict the goodness of God, God asks us to listen to the voice of God. If we decide to listen to the voice of God, we'll hear the Good News. God is with us in encounters that make no positive sense.

Dietrich Bonhoeffer and Spiritual Sensitivity

During World War II evangelicals in Germany formed the Confessing Church. They opposed the German Christian Church movement sponsored by the Nazis from 1932 until 1945. As Nazi influence increased the Confessing Church was forced to go underground. In 1935 the confessing church formed a seminary near Zingst on the Baltic Sea.

A 29-year-old pastor and professor, Dietrich Bonhoeffer led the students in a disciplined life together. Those seminarians knew they were living on the edge of eternity. Those were days of longsuffering. Nazis finally closed the seminary in 1937. The students of the seminary were arrested.

In March of 1943, Bonhoeffer participated in an attempt to kill Adolph Hitler. On April 5, he was arrested. He had shared two books, *Life Together* and *The Cost of Discipleship*. He was tortured and humiliated, suffered everything imaginable for two long years. On April 9, 1945, he was hanged by the Gestapo in a concentration camp at the age of 39. Hebrews 3:12.

Bonhoeffer was a highly sensitive person filled with Spirit given longsuffering. He was ablaze with love. Saints who persevere until the finish will be saved. Hebrews 10:23-25. The closer we get to the end of our days or perhaps the Second Coming. Eternal security is a community project. Sensitive believers need to meet together. Meet in homes, in restaurants, meet underground if you have to because of circumstances. We need not have just glib conversation. Concentrate every word with the Word of God and prayer.

Sensitive souls will profit from travel to a distant sate or even a foreign country rather than endure the wrath of insensitive persons as the Nazis were. We can weigh our decisions to ensure they are making the right ones. We understand much more than others the consequences of our choices. It is best not to choose in light of the current pressure to be rushed.

Longsuffering people are hard on themselves.

When a Spirit-filled person makes a mistake or realizes they have done something wrong, they hurt themselves. They feel so bad about how te chose to act in certain encounters. We are empathetic toward others, even those we encountered with the best intentions to bring joy not suffering into their lives.

Longsuffering people are their worst critics. Their purpose is for perfection in all they do. The positive thing is that they are self-aware. They learn from each encounter whether it was bad or good. If someone betrays them. It is incredibly hard. They think t is impossible to move on. We are gracious to forgive, they know the most effective boundaries. Our inner child lives on even as we get older. To leave a super sensitive person hanging in what has been perceived in a vulnerable encounter has harrowing effects and brings on a crushed world. With grace and compassion, we put ourselves in other shoes and we do not lose love of ourselves or cherished others.

We are always enriched by positive encounters. Our hearts are open when we find the joy that is eternal. Outside forces might limit or even end your times of cherished encounters, but nothing can destroy real love.

Super Sensitive People and Self-esteem

We all have levels of self-esteem. In painful encounters, they desire to avoid all confrontation. They have always done everything they think of to keep the peace.

They have a child-like innocence about them. They are super aware of themselves and their own feelings than the normal average person. It is detrimental when others are brutally honest which is their choice to be mean-spirited. Word choice, body language and tone of voice will be noticed and thought over and over again Jesus was a super sensitive empath. Because Jesus was God incarnated, he was able to empathize with all people, no matter what their personality or background. We see this as we read the gospel story in scripture. I do not mean to say that the other 16 personality types in the Myers-Briggs Personality Indicator are never empathetic.

The gospels do not make it completely clear whether Jesus was sensitive to smell, sight, light, sound or taste. When Jesus ministered to large groups, we are aware that he pulled away from some of these groups by getting in a boat as a way to get away. He needed alone time to regroup. Being like Jesus, they have profound spiritual and intuitive experiences. Jesus had these qualities. He was able to sense the needs and thoughts of those around him before they said a word.

When Jesus was baptized, the sky opened up. A voice declared him as a beloved son. During the transfiguration with Peter, James, and John, his appearance was transformed before them. They even heard Jesus talk with Moses and Elijah, who were there.

Life is difficult to navigate for anybody. With constant stimulation coming from each experience, humans must find a way to shield themselves from the energy of others. Jesus knew how to do this s he cast out demons with his authority. Jesus was perfect in his sensitivity to others. This is the prime reason that billions of followers throughout human history have followed Christ.

Our potential is infinite.

I respect the inner work it takes to embody our nature and the best character and person. Our potential self is infinite. I also admire the dedication needed to break free of conformity. I am delighted to know conscious highly sensitives that understands that we are all energy.

Our empathetic receptivity gives us the ability to be in extended conversation with God and those we encounter in the environment of this world.

We can all create a list of physical sensations that communicate information to us. Explore meditations that offer stillness to reset our minds.

"Highly sensitive people are easy to love and easy to live with as long as you try to meet their unique needs."

Jennifer Granneman

Chapter Eight
Longsuffering and Forgiveness

When we encounter relationships that are close, they draw out the best and worst of us. Love is never flawless. Loving is blinding. We refuse the real picture. Fragile human love becomes fatal. The couple eventually may see the other person as for our personal enjoyment. We love them for who they are. People are sensitive and insecure cling to each other. We need to respect ourselves.

A lack of forgiveness comes in many forms. Resentment takes root in unexpected breakups or betrayal. Longsuffering times are needed for letting go of the past hurt and to heal. Our decision to forgive will ultimately lead a joyous fulfilling life.

Universally, every person on earth has been wronged by somebody. Forgiving a person who has wronged us is never easy, but dwelling on these events and reliving them over and over can fill the mind with negative thoughts and suppressed anger." (Tyler VanderWeele, "The Power of Forgiveness," *Harvard Health*, p. 44.

Forgiveness is decisional and emotional. Decisional forgiveness means making a conscious choice to replace hurt with wishing only good things will happen to the one whom you encountered.

Emotional forgiveness means to move away from negative feelings and to stop dwelling on the wrongdoing. Without both types of forgiveness, negative and unhealthy depression, anxiety, hostility, and substance abuse. Life will not be satisfying.

When you find yourself wondering where to begin, forgive yourself first. Longsuffering will help you do that. Martin Luther taught us to maintain the capacity to forgive. He said, "One who is devoid of love is devoid of the power to love." I have come to realize that forgiveness is the way to love. Resentment, retaliation, and revenge destroys our capacity for love. The natural instinct is to pay back evil for evil.

To become more comfortable with forgiveness, practice small acts. Start with something as trivial as cutting you off in traffic and realizing it was not directed to you personally. Forgive on the spot.

Without an unconditional commitment, there is no way for us to live in eternal life. Sort out any damaged relationships. Confess that you did not do it right and acknowledge the mistakes and faults. Ultimately only the offer to apologize and forgive will heal all people involved. Forgiving people ensures that everyone involved has the ability to live with all things in the past. Pray for the grace to forgive. Matthew 18:22.

Withholding forgiveness causes all to suffer and we are the losers. We are released from the encounter. Forgiveness is that important.

Forgiveness might not produce effective reconciliation. Time and patience are essential. Forgiveness is a complex thing. When King James had the Bible translated into English, the translator used "forgive us our debts as we forgive our debtors."

When the Lord's Prayer was first translated into English it was rendered as "forgive our trespasses as e forgive those who trespass against us." Many use the word "sin" as both debts and trespasses are not clear. By forgiveness, God disinfects the hidden places in our memories in which there is still resentment. Nursing grudges destroys us. Years in the past we heard a popular recording of the spiritual "O Happy Day." It was upbeat music. Its sound attracted people. "O Happy Day, the day that Jesus washed my sins away." Christ accomplished just what we need to know forgiveness. We never ever have to concerned by our encounters with sin.

Forgiven people keep running the race. They overcome temptation. They have a clear conscience. All our past is gone forever. We are debt free.

Dying people fully realize it's vital to forgive and let go of old hurts. Letting go makes it possible to get on with life. Forgiveness is not a natural response to being wronged. Forgiving another for a serious wrong is the most difficult thing to do.

Forgiveness is the core of our faith. To be in relationship with God, we must have the willingness to forgive. An effective way to cultivate a forgiving spirit is to get into the habit of forgiveness. Forgiving takes humility. We admit that we were wrong. We give up self-control.

Self-forgiveness is the foundation.

Look into your mirror and contemplate some of the hurts that you have responsibility for. The foundational issue is self-forgiveness. We have goodness and good qualities, but we do not focus on them. We think that we will never get things right. We regret the choices we have made. Our sins may not have been as damaging and dramatic as others.

Genuine forgiveness for serious wrongs is rare. Let us look at the joy of forgiveness. As God forgives us and as we know our own forgiveness, to feel blessed by everything, even by those who have hurt us. Great is the faithfulness of God to save us. This is beyond all our empirical and felt experiences. It is based on the promise of Jesus who has shown himself to be a faithful witness on our behalf. After all, Jesus being God, was the reason he could be so forgiving. His faithfulness must have once been beyond mystery, beyond any human understanding.

His forgiveness is the epitome of eternal joy.

The Joy of Forgiveness

As a writer bringing joy to the world, this work would not be complete without words on the joy of forgiveness. Psalm 32:1-2. The psalm begins with a declaration of forgiveness and its blessedness. To be absolved of guilt is to enter the kingdom of God. Sin is covered by salvation.

We are justified by Christ by our faith. Ultimately, forgiveness rescues us from the wrath of God. In the days of the psalmist, rain ebbs and flows down the mountains to produce streams of water. During the dry season, these riverbeds will be dried out.

When the next rainy season happens, flash floods fill the wadis when water flows suddenly and rushes into the dry channels. Without forgiveness, our souls are dried up. Repentance is a life-long process with longsuffering leading to joy.

What joy to be in right relationship with God. Psalm 32:5-6. We have been given freedom by the Holy Spirit. We will receive blessings beyond our imagination.

We shall rejoice when Christ comes again. We do not know the full essence of how this will be. He is coming in the present time when we accept the living Christ to live in us. The prophet Isaiah gives the coming Messiah dramatic flavor. Isaiah 25:6-12.

We hunger for love, grace, pace, and God's amazing gifts that leads us to the anticipation of "the day of the Lord." Imagine the day of the Lord as a cosmic wedding feast that brings together the bride and the groom together. Mercy shines bright and glorious. The pleasures we have been blessed with in this world can become a window to he glory found in heaven.

It will be a day full of joy. This joy is a surprise package that rings us to the point of passion and gratitude. Our missing the mark, our mistakes, and wrong understanding cannot be erased with nothing being done. The joy of our forgiveness brings even a greater strength to a relationship. The passion of our Father is to weave glory out of brokenness.

God smiles with joy as we do the smallest kindness, a rewarding goodness, a grace, small expressions of love, all the effects of joy. Hebrews 13:15-16.

God is pleased. God nods the head when we give a cup of cold water. We live out the themes of our individual stories and bring joys to our little corner of the world. We all live with burdens that we cannot escape. To neglect our burden is to lose our soul.

God has shaped each of those who are called children. The Creator of all people leads us into situations and encounters that reflects God's glory and love.

In our times of longsuffering, we appear to be strange and unpredictable. We fit in with the others as we persevere. We cannot be dismissed from love. We who begin the healing path will be reconciled and fully healed and sanctified.

We walk the redemption path all alone. God woos us with his mysterious love. We travel with a few others. Our community is vital. Hebrews 3:12- 13, 10:23-25. In our longsuffering we are living in drying cement. We must endure with patience on our journey or we will become bound and enslaved to someone or something strange other than God.

We come together at the local well, in the coffee shop, at school events, on riverbanks to find our strength in the joy of the Lord. The Day of the Lord will come soon. Even if it does not come for another millennium, it is soon.

We need visionaries who will plunge into the unknown and mysterious. We need people who in the Holy Spirit can interpret our times. We need those who will encourage us. The experience of consolation following an encounter is a sign that this was the will of our Lord God. The encounter initially was at odds with our personal preference.

Our own will becomes the will of God. The Spirit of God has joined our spirit. This indeed could take time. We must be in contact with our deepest self and become quiet before the Lord.

Longsuffering takes on a vision quest with others who serve a vision, who serve each other and the glory of God.

"If we really want to love, we must learn to forgive." Mother Teresa

Chapter Nine
Longsuffering and Retirement

Retirement taught me that to love some difficult people. Some days I have experienced the best job and at times the worst. Wedding rehearsals is the meeting of two families similar to Scottish clans ready for a fight. Preaching grace becomes a work for the minister.

Scripture teaches that humans are geared to live 70 years tops. Psalm 90:10. In my eighties, I was aware of that, Even with small retirement money, it has been difficult to pay the mortgage, looking after frail relatives and parents. Now most of them have died. Many. People die after just two years of retirement is disturbing and part of our longsuffering. Retirees now on pension and social security react to suddenly stopping and adjusting to a new unfamiliar pattern of living.

Some will just give up and die because they have no vision or purpose in staying alive. If we are not busy and still accomplishing, we act as if all life has been completed. We fail to recognize the good things we enjoy such as using our gifts and hearing our children and grandchildren tell us that they love us.

Retirees see themselves winding down with no vision quest for the transition years. Resisting change is an option. Inertia makes few demands. Change can provoke us into a new life. It takes tons of energy to end the race well.

Our transitions were never stress-free. Our clock keeps ticking in the background. Our bones ache, our vision and our senses decline. So some press the deep freeze button. Retirees live with physical suffering, which gives the opportunity for the grace of God to bring comfort. We might feel inadequate. We will be made complete. Our severe trails causes us to be desperate for the deliverance of God. II Corinthians 1:8.

If our life partner is still living, the other will retreat within feeling confused. If they are living, we have to encounter our spouse every single day. Both need space. Retirement has the power to sharpen our hold on life. Retirees may doubt their self-worth. They need to create new visions and goals. John 10:10. Joy is ours in our later years as in our time of youth.

Retirement transition involve letting go and moving on. We accept our losses and gains. Ever joyful in her longsuffering, Helen Keller advised, "One should never count the years. One's should count one's interests. I have kept young, trying never to lose my childhood sense of wonder. I am glad I still have a vivid curiosity about the world I live in."

Wise retirees need to resist the fantasy of wanting to be somebody else. Some choose to live in retirement years in a denominational care center. For Catholics, a monastery regulates each day. These settings allow time for solitude and for joining others in the community for relaxation or recreation. Retirement is a time of rich fulfillment, an opportunity to achieve more than we can imagine. Retirees are capable of immense creativity. We need not miss the joys of later life.

Christ's relationship with his Father secures for us a similar relationship with our God of mercies and comfort. Both our sufferings and comforts are experienced in abundance.

God has not promised to keep out of the furnace of trials. God pledged to be with us in the fire all the years of our lives. No believer is alone in hard times. God is there beside us.

We will never understand fully why we must experience suffering. The pain hurts because it is how we discover what God can do. Never attempt to run from pain. Face up to it as pain renews the strengthening of God. Suffering breaks the stubborn spirit of self-will within us that insists on using our own resources. Suffering shows us that we are not alone in life. We are members of a family. We are members of a Body. The outcome is patient endurance. Joy surprises us when we experience the sufficiency of God in times of suffering. Therefore, we do not resent affliction but we are honored, as suffering for Christ is not a curse, but a blessing. God used the suffering of Jesus to forgive our sins.

Suffering is not something we seek. It is something we accept, knowing it comes from God. II Corinthians 4:7. Christ honors the integrity of commitment. Christ is the ultimate standard. Christ fulfills all of the promises of God.

God's love experiences profound grief when beloved people fall into disloyalty and error. There is a connection between the faithfulness of God and our ability to make and keep commitments with integrity. Psalm 15:4.

During my own retirement years, I have been privileged to write books and preach in places nobody else wants to encounter. We can always learn something new. On my own tombstone I would ask for the words "Minister of Joy to the World" to be there for all to see.

During our retirement years, we become re-enchanted with wonder. We are not obsessed by what we do not have. We miss the joy of having friends, the beauty of nature, even hearing the grass grow. Isaiah 55:2.

During retreats with fellow associations for retired ministers, I love to go out for a walk or just sit, observe, and reflect. I have hundreds of rocks from places I have enjoyed with the date and place written on the stones. On a visit to Bethesda, Maryland, my daughter shared her own rock collection of the places she has enjoyed.

Those rock collections give us a sense of journey of where we came from and where we would like to be. The older we become, the more precious becomes our experiences. We cherish the events that shaped us for good. We find ourselves contemplating the opportunities we missed and the mistakes we have made.

The Bible tells us that sharing our memories is a spiritual obligation. Deuteronomy 4:9. Our stories shape our present living. Some end their lives frail and isolated. Communities and churches have long memories. Mostly a group will re-enact during a crisis. We have to accept each other's memories in good faith, recognizing how it was for them. Leave it at that.

We will never experience contentment if we are not at peace with our past encounters. Longsuffering and forgiveness is a painful process. These are necessary for change. Life is too brief to postpone them.

A new quality of life can begin at any hour of any day only if we choose to live now and to live creatively. Age is not a factor. God has anointed us. Norman Vincent Peale anointed me as the Minister of Joy to the World. The New Testament speaks about anointing in I John 2:20, 27.

God anointed believers and followers for us to be prepared and empowered to serve our Lord. Forgiveness and restoration are at the heart of ministry from our calling in the beginning to the state of retirement. Forgiveness is part of the essence of God. God stands ready to forgive. A forgiving spirit never counts the number of times that a person has sinned. Forgiveness is always extended to someone who does not feel she or he deserves it.

The salvation accomplished by Christ cannot be stressed enough. Knowledge of Christ is a sweet aroma that permeates those around us and accomplishes the purposes of God in the lives of those we touch. Inward transformation is to have a mature Christlikeness. II Corinthians 4:18.

God is ultimately glorified.

The ministry of the gospel is not easy. It is not even possible in our own strength. The fragrance is invisible. "Fragrance and aroma are excellent figures of speech.

Jesus came to change our hearts, to transform us from the inside out. Initial conversion plays out in ongoing sanctification by the Spirit so that our increasing Christlikeness is evident. Being saved means our convictions and conversions are possible though the Word of God and the Holy Spirit. The world cannot help but to notice.

Righteousness means to be fully accepted, having a sense of being approved by God. God gives us a standing of worth.

Christ Jesus came preaching as he reconciled u to God our Father, who has granted us free access and boldness to approach the throne of grace. Christ filled us with confidence toward God. The opposite of boldness is fear or timidity. Boldness does not indicate shame. The Spirit give us the courage to be unashamed. Boldness is open frank, direct, straightforward, and plain speech concerning the things of God. John 10:24.

Plain means bold. Boldness overcomes the temptation to conceal the truth wit vagueness. People who are not bold or confident are unsure of themselves. They are insecure. They travel the journey of life and never make a good impression on anyone. They are always failing and losing.

Faithful and longsuffering servants get discouraged and lose heart.

The face attacks against their character, the legitimacy of their anointed ministry, and denial of the effectiveness of their ministry.

The way we view our ministries will help determine how to fulfill it. When ministry become a burden instead of a privilege, it is easy to quit. Faithfull ministers have the tendency and habit to keep on serving Christ regardless of the circumstances, regardless of what others have said about them, and regardless of anyone responding in the way the servant wanted them to respond.

Integrity is the ultimate safeguard against discouragement. Lack of results do not distract from the preciousness or the effectiveness. The focus should never be on ourselves. The first thing some ministers do upon retirement is to write a book of memoirs praising themselves.

In every age for ministry, the focus must be on the glory of Christ. Christ supremely reveals the image of God. Olde and younger people must gaze intently into the face of Christ.

Retirement gives us the extreme opportunity to find other new ways to do ministry. Physical challenges will not distract the retired minister from their eternal focus. Suffering affliction with perseverance requires focusing on the eternal weight of glory.

It is a longsuffering adjustment when we retire. In the beginning, we might feel that we have escaped the daily grind, the long commute, difficult bosses. We miss the sense of meaning, purpose, and integrity that came with your work.

Instead of feeling free, relaxed, and fulfilled, we feel depressed, aimless, and isolated. Retiring from work is a major life change. Retirement is linked with declining health. Those living in their first year of retirement are about 50 per cent more likely to suffer a heart attack or stroke than those who keep working.

Whatever your circumstances, ending work life brings challenges. Struggling to switch off from working and just relax leads to feeling anxious. Some find it difficult to fill their extra hours with meaningful activity. We think we have lost our identity. When we are no longer a pastor, a doctor, an engineer, or a teacher, we ask, "Who am I now?"

Aged ones, be patient.

We learn from those who travel the road of faith before us. Growing older, we become aware that others are watching and imitating us. Let others see your wrinkle and warts and struggles. Titus 2:1-2. (Sarah Hornsby, *The Fruit of the Spirit*, p. 227-228)

Coping with change is not easy. The older we get life changes at an ever- quickening rate. We will have to change our attitude as retirement becomes a sacred journey rather than a destination. Build resilience. We can improve the qualities of resiliency if we have the courage.

Accept that longsuffering in retirement is a reality. Resisting or denial is fatal. Refocus energy to things we have no control over.

We must set new goals to discover a new sense of purpose and a redefining of identity. Reaching out and sharing the burden helps ease stress. We are never too old to build rewarding and new friendships. Part time work can ease the pain, keep us socially engaged without the demands of full-time work.

"Do not go where the path may lead. Go instead where there is no path and leave a trail."

Ralph Waldo Emerson

Chapter Ten
Longsuffering and Death

Death is a terrifying reality. Hebrews 9:27. Death is frightening.

Death is not really the end. The terrifying is especially for those living outside the Christian faith. Hebrews 12:14-15.

When a person dies, normal people ask, "What happens in death? Is there an afterlife? What is our purpose? How do we go on living? "We are not alone in our pain. We will relive the spiritual experiences of our life journey. These moments can take our breath away. Spirituality affects our senses. We shall transcend our fears with new strength and freedom. Bereavement is like a longsuffering journey. We travel from a place to another place to call home.

A Russian Orthodox minister wrote: "Death is the most profound and significant fact of life. It lifts the last of the mortals above the darkness and banality of life. Only the fact of death puts the question of life's meaning. Meaning is linked with ending. If there were no end, there would be no meaning to life." David Rankin, *My Ending Is My Beginning*, p. 28.

We deny death's reality. When a loved one dies, we call the funeral home, and an undertaker prepares the body for the casket or cremation. Experiencing another's death is the way we find meaning in the death of ourselves. If we don't have intimate experiences with dying people, we can't know the meaning of death. Longsuffering shows that we have been dying from birth.

This book is not about life after death. It is a book about life and death. Not life later, but life now as life in this life. Saint Francis said in his prayer, "It is in dying that we live."

To begin to understand life, we must understand our dying. Facing death raises questions. Elizabeth Kubler-Ross wrote, "Death is the key to the door of life." Elizabeth Kubler-Ross, *Death, the Final Stage of Growth*, pp. 67-68. Contemplating our death reveals what is really important.

Grief happens to us. We simply respond. Grief cannot be controlled. We live with trouble and suffering. We are overwhelmed by the emotions we will experience. Grief responds to the rhythms of our soul.

Death is uncomfortable. We do not know what to say. We can't think of ways to be helpful. Unless we have gone through a similar death, we do not know how another feels. Presence is more important than insight. Focus on giving support and care. Loved ones are letting go a little bit at a time.

Only God has the tools for conquering death. Only God can use miraculous power for overcoming death. Eternal almighty power and the resurrection of the son of God. Death is the gateway to eternity.

Death always comes as a shock. Longsuffering has given us time to prepare. Death always comes too soon. Death comes at he wrong time. Death draws us up short. Pain and grief, separation, emptiness, and heartache are the names of the suffering that death brings.

Tears come from deep within us to cleanse and to lead us to the fresh waters of life.

But for now, they are shocked. In grieving, they are struggling with frightening thoughts and unwanted feelings. They feel afraid and even guilty. They feel despair and rage. Confusion and forgetfulness causes the grieving to think that they are losing their minds. Their longsuffering pain is not like any other pain. In reality, life will never be the same before death entered our space.

Loss is always bittersweet. We cannot know its sting without having known the bliss of love. We intensely felt the loss when we spot someone who looks like my brother at a football game. I see her in the romantic movies and my feelings do a double flip. I catch a whiff of her perfume, and I hear a song that we hummed together.

Death is our last enemy as the apostle Paul writes in I Corinthians 15-26. Every person living on earth today will die. Hebrews 9:27. Death keeps women and men in states of fear.

Elizabeth Kubler-Ross specialized in research on death and dying. She said, "It is only when we truly know and understand that we have a limited time on earth, and that we have no way of knowing when our time is up that we begin to live each day to the full, as if it were the only day we had."

Death is our finale. Quantity of years does not equate to the quality of life. In those final years we suffer from frailty, cracking bones, hearing loss, declining sight, failing heath, decreased mobility, and memory problems. Our finale deals with the longsuffering because of our weaknesses. It is frustrating not to be able to do simple things. It is tough growing old.

Older people become isolated. They become lonely. They are rarely physically touched. There is so little affection, affirmation, or love. It is disastrous to most. Those who have to give up driving their automobile and stopping driving to and from feels helpless.

Living in a care center with people you have not chosen is a bitter pill to swallow. Just having some company is not the same as warm companionships. John 21:18. Being filled with the fruit of the Spirit takes away our fear of death. Death really is our last enemy. As we trust our faithfulness in Jesus, despite our many sins, we can rejoice in Romans 8:31-39.

I get inspired by those to be soon departed. Look at those you encounter and tell them that you love them. If you think you do not love them, try to understand, and then forgive and love them. The idea of a hospice was created in London, England. Today's hospice is filled with young and old, but mostly people full of years. Many are in grievous pain and have suffered long. Some lived in the fog of pain killing drugs. They have decided to accept their looming death as unavoidable.

Healing takes time. Healing demands a sensitive quiet attitude toward those who have lost and grieved.

The living can benefit from the wisdom of the dying. One purpose for writing this book is to remind ourselves that life is short. Every day counts. Those dying live in the present rather than focusing on the past or fretting about their future.

Most are grateful for the life they lived. Given the pain these people were facing and all that they must leave behind. Joy is found in those things that have always been there.

The hope of heaven gave people joy. They looked forward to heaven but they had enjoyed the blessings of this life. They have already tasted heaven and living has been a fantastic journey.

When looming death comes, two words say it all: "Being loved." Things that bring joy to people were readily available. Our vision quest to joy does not require us to make long journeys. We are surrounded by joy.

Facing eternity, they turn their focus on what is stronger than death— love. Spiritual sensitivity is enhanced by the nearness of death.

We feel helpless and hopeless when a person we love is sick or dying. We think we can do nothing. We can show up and pray. We can use our phone or send an email. We can't take it with us. Earthly treasures rust and corrupt. Everything must be left behind.

Dying people feel grateful for a slow death, rather than a sudden and unexpected departure. They are able to tie up loose ends, to say the things they wanted to say. They are free from the need to continually look into the future.

Life happens in the present time. When my lovely wife Laurel got the diagnosis of cancer, both she and I decided that we were going to live our lives as fully and completely as possible. Unforgiveness brings unbelievable harm to your health. Living in the future will not make the suffering any less. Continuing to dwell on the future will not how us overcome the lingering bad feelings toward someone who did those wrong things to us.

Living in the future brings disappointment.

When we miss out on the present, we are kept from enjoying now. Those joys of living in the present is that it leaves us open to surprises and mysteries of the future.

A wise woman said, "Make your plans, but don't pack your bags too early. You'll miss the abundance of life." Enjoy every moment for we do know when life will end. Life is a brief time. We do with our times of life is our choice. Choosing how to life is never easy.

Living in the present is a matter of taking advantage of life's simple pleasures. One of my wise elders said, "I came into this world to die. We should not be surprised when our time arrives. We have to live expecting and believing we are going to die."

Reconciliation and Forgiveness

To be reconciled with others, we must be willing to forgive and to ask for forgiveness. Sometimes reconciliation is difficult because both involved feel that they were mostly right or mostly wrong. So the stand-off continues. Our pride and embarrassment become immovable barriers. All parties must believe that they are responsible. During the longsuffering days of the encounter, we know we cannot meet people halfway. Grace is involved and reconciliation is important.

Happiness and eternal joy are elusive, but these ae as near as our loved ones. Be proactive as you seek love. Love covers a multitude of sins." I Peter 4:8. As I write this book, love, grace, and joy is coming toward me from every direction. Love is given and love is received. Joy is newly defined as being loved. Love never fails.

The light of God's love never stops glowing. And that light helps us through the longsuffering of our early lives in a whole new vision. In the end the love of God banishes all regrets.

Into every life, a little rain must fall.

Regrets and disappointments come in the lost joy-filled people. Managing life with unhappy circumstances requires spiritual perception. Life does not always quite the way we want. Longsuffering brings sensitive people see the big picture. Our encounters are balanced with the good things in life.

When our time of death is fully realized, we do not speak of regretting not living our lives differently. Soon departing people define failure and success differently.

Nothing is more important than relationships. They were proud that they loved more and deeply, even if the love just died and would never be finished. Humans are relational beings. One of the surprising things I have heard is people saying, "I married the wrong person." People report that they stay in unhappy marriages for years. Some report that they should have their spouses because there was so much suffering." How said their stories of brokenness are. Too late in life—just too late.

The great news is that God redeems our mistakes. Painful longsuffering arouses by events beyond our control. It may be too late to fix or repair them. The time will come when it is too late. Listen to the voices of those who are dying. The closer and enjoyable the connection may have been and still is, the more intense the pain will be.

The fire of our anguish

Death is scary. We fear for our immortality. Nothing extinguishes the fire. Remember the light they left in the world. I and my world is better because they were in it. The memories cause us to smile.

The fire of grief is a peculiar thing. We are so helpless. Sadness overcomes us and we can do nothing to ease it. Longsuffering has many benefits that are unspeakable.

We must run the whole race of life well. The joy of the Lord is a permanent gift. God will never cease to hold us close. The joy of the Lord is our strength.

Funerals and memorial services are for the living not the dead. Ritual is important. They remind us that the dead remain alive and significant. Sharing food after a memorial service is wonderful.

Tears and laughter flow during the reception. There is a place for humor in the after the time of death. Laughter does not replace our grieving. We will live on by our words and deeds. These will have a ripple effect.

I am willing, even content to sit with the mystery of death. My love for you is mine, and your love for me is yours. What remains is a shadow. We can no longer hug our loved ones. We will no longer make love. We will not share meals together. We did not have the opportunity to say good- bye. Death cannot take love away. Love's fire will never go out.

Keep on fanning the flames to restore the way it used to be. Memories will remain forever. They are ingrained in our souls where love resides. Luke 24:44-53.

Albert Einstein was brilliant. As many smart people, his head was usually in the clouds. His wife said where Einstein was walking down the street to his house, he would walk into the wrong door. His wife painted the door to their home bright red. One day a newspaper reporter asked her if she know the theory of relativity. She said, "No I don't, but I know Albert. That's all I need to know."

In the end, the important thing is knowing Jesus Christ as a continuing presence. Knowing Christ beyond the limits of time and space as an eternal spiritual force at work in us, through us, and beyond us. What's left is what matters.

Heaven is far beyond our imagination. I Corinthians 2:9. Heaven is life without negatives. There are no thieves breaking through to steal. There is no fading, losing, aging, or dying. Rust and moths are not there. This is the day we decide that we will live the rest of our journey on earth as citizens of heaven. Revelation 21:3-4.

Nothing can separate us from the love of God. Love is a tangible reality. It is born of devotion or passion. Love demands work and sacrifice. When we live for love, we will meet every challenge that crosses our pathway, even the final one—death. If we live our lives in love, we will know joy and peace now, as well as the hour of our death. (Johann Christoph Arnold, *Watch for the Light*, p. 157.)

"To ask of death that it never come is futile, but is not futility to pray that when death comes

for us, it may take us from a world one corner of which is a little better because we were there."

Jacob Rudin

Bibliography

Arndt, William. *A Greek-English Lexicon of the New Testament and Other Early Christian Literature.* Chicago: University of Chicago Press, 1979.

Arnold, Johann Christoph. *Watch for the Light.* Maryknoll, New York: Plough Publishing Company, 2008.

Asselin, David. "Christian Maturity and Spiritual Discernment," *Review for Religious.* Vol. 27, pp. 581-595, 1968.

Barclay, William. *The Daily Bible Series.* Philadelphia: The Westminster Press, 1854.

Brice, Peter: On the Edge: *Wrestling with God in Depression.* Norwich, England: Millstream Press, 1995.

Brooks, David. *The Road to Character.* New York: Random House, 2015.

Brooks, David. *The Second Mountain: The Quest for a Moral Life.* New York: Random House, 2020.

Christenson, Evelyn. *Changing Your Life Through the. Power of Prayer.* New York: Inspirational Press, 1980.

Chopra, Deepak. *Ageless Body Timeless Mind.* New York: Harmony Books, 1993.

Cole, Thomas. *The Journey of Life: A Cultural History of Aging in America.* Cambridge: Cambridge University Press, 1992.

Day, Dorothy. *The Long Loneliness: The Autobiography of the Legendary Catholic Social Activist.* San Francisco: Harper and Row, 1952.

Davids, Peter. *Commentary on James.* Grand Rapids, Michigan: Eerdmans Publishing Company, 1984.

Douglas, J.D., organizing editor. New Bible Dictionary. Wheaton, Illinois: Tyndale House, 1992.

Downs, Hugh. *Fifty to Forever.* Nashville: Thomas Nelson, 1994.

Dulles, Avery. "Finding God's Will," Woodstock Letters, pp. 139-140, Spring edition, 1970.

Ellul, Jacques. *Hope in a Time of Abandonment*. New York: Seabury Press, 1973.

Forest, Jim. *All Is Grace: A Biography of Dorothy Day*. New York: Orbus Press, 2011.

Hauser, Richard J. *In His Spirit: A Guide to Today's Spirituality*. New York: Paulist Press, 1989.

Jewell, Albert. *Spirituality and Aging*. London: Jessica Kingsley Publishers, 2004.

Killinger, John. *Bread for the Wilderness, Wine for the Journey*. Waco, Texas: Word Books, 1976.

Killinger, John. *The Gospel of Contagious Joy: A Devotional Guide to Luke*. Waco, Texas: Word Books, 1980.

Knight, George. *Servant Theology in Isaiah 40-55*. Grand Rapids, Michigan: International Publishers, 1998.

Kubler-Ross, Elizabeth. *Death, the Final Sage of Growth*. New York: Touchstone, 1975.

Levinas, Emanuel. *Ethics and Infinity*. Gloucester, Massachusetts: Peter Smith Publishing Company, 1978.

Lewis, C.S. *The Weight of Glory*. New York: Harper, 1976.

Louw, Johannes and Eugene Nida, editors. *Greek-English Lexicon of the New Testament*. New York: United Bible Societies, 1989.

Mays, James L., editor. *Harper's Bible Commentary*. San Francisco: Harper and Row, 1988.

McReynolds, James. *Black Preaching: Burden of a People*. Nashville: self-published, 1972.

McReynolds, James. *Fighting for the Faith*. London: United Kingdom Free Press, 1999.

McReynolds, James. *Grace Revealed: Bringing Joy to the World*. Cleveland, Tennessee: Parson's Porch Books, 2022.

McReynolds, James. *The Joy of Prayer: The Way to Intimacy with God*. Cleveland, Tennessee: Parson's Porch Books, 2017.

McReynolds, James. *Walking in the Garden with God*. Cleveland,

Tennessee, 2021.

Mitchell, Henry. *Soul Theology*. San Francisco: Harper and Row, 1977.

Nouwen, Henri. *The Inner Voice of Love*. New York: Image Books, 1999.

Oden, Marilyn Brown. *Abundance: Joyful Living in Christ*. Nashville: Upper Room Books, 2004.

Packer, J. I. *Concise Theology*. Wheaton, Illinois: Tyndale House, 1996.

Pogue, Bekah Jane. *Choosing Real: An Invitation to Celebrate When Life Doesn't Go as Planned*. Uhrichsville, Ohio: Shiloh Run Press, 2016.

Rankin, David. *My Ending Is My Beginning*. Grand Rapids, Michigan: Fountain Street Publishers, 1999.

Saint Romain, Philip. *The Logic of Happiness: Proverbs and Practical Wisdom for Spiritual Living*. Liguori, Missouri: Triumph Publishing Company, 1996.

Shianabarger, Jeffrey. *Yes and No: How Your Everyday Decisions Will Forever Shape Your life*. Colorado Springs, Colorado: David C. Cook Publishers, 2014.

Sittser, Jerry. *A Grace Disguised: How the Soul Grows through Loss*. Grand Rapids, Michigan: Zondervan Publishing Company, 2004.

Tournier, Paul. *The Seasons of Life*. Richmond, Virginia: John Knox Press, 1963.

Underhill, Evelyn. *Mysticism: A Study in the Nature and Development of Man's Spiritual Consciousness*. New York: New American Library Press, 2022.

Vanderweele, Tyler, "The Power of Forgiveness," February 12, 2021, *Harvard Health*. Cambridge, Massachusetts: Harvard Health Publishing, 2021.

Van deWalle, Janet. "Save Your Life! They Are Stealing More Than Joy," *Women's Edition*, p. 64, November 2023.

Willard, Dallas. *The Spirit of the Disciplines: Understanding How God Changes*. San Francisco: Harper, 1988.

Williamson, H. W. "Sound, Sense, and Language in Isaiah 24-27," *Journal of Jewish Studies*, pp. 1-9, 1999.

Williamson, Marianne. *Everyday Grace: Having Hopes, Finding Forgiveness, and Making Miracles*. Houston, Texas: Riverhead Books, 2022.

About the Author